JOURNEY TO THE END OF THE WORLD

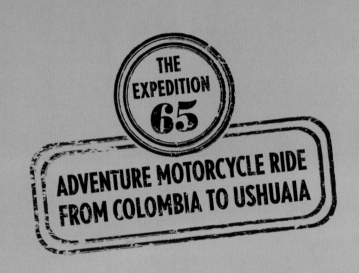

THE
EXPEDITION
65

ADVENTURE MOTORCYCLE RIDE
FROM COLOMBIA TO USHUAIA

JOURNEY TO THE END OF THE WORLD

ALFONSE PALAIMA & COLIN EVANS

OCTANE PRESS

The idea for Expedition 65 came while I was on a lonely road leading our Continental Divide-South America tour in October of 2014. I'd like to dedicate this book to the guys and gals who rode with me on that tour: Rob W, John, Steve, Colin, Rob J, Mike, Doug, Dave, Agnes, Charlie, Maria, and Michael. Thanks for being part of the inspiration for the greatest adventure of my life!

—*Jim Hyde*

Octane Press, First Edition
October 2017
© 2017 by Alfonse Palaima and Colin Evans

ISBN: 978-1-937747-85-5

Cover and Interior Design by John Barnett | 4eyesdesign.com
Edited by Andrew Cherney
Proofread by Dana Henricks

On the endpapers: Expedition Preparation © 2016. Credit Alfonse Palaima
On the frontispiece: Racing across the Salar de Uyuni. © 2016. Credit Alfonse Palaima
On the title page: Ibid

OCTANE
PRESS

octanepress.com

CONTENTS

6. CENTRAL ANDES

7. PATAGONIA

8. EPILOGUE

Our journey down the length of South America spanned 65 degrees of latitude and more than a dozen crossings of the Andes mountains.

FOREWORD

All grand schemes usually begin with an epiphany, and Expedition 65 was no exception.

I was leading a group of riders out to the Uyuni Salt Flats in Bolivia on our first "Continental Divide of South America" tour, and we had about half an hour to capture the mandatory "been there, done that" photos before hightailing it to the evening's destination. Suddenly it hit me—here I am in one of the most remarkable places on earth, and I've got 30 minutes to soak it all up before we have to haul ass to the next stop. I decided right there that I needed to do a trip where I could slow down and explore the Uyuni in a more leisurely manner. And the idea for Expedition 65 was born.

As the owner of RawHyde Adventures and BMW's off-road rider training center, I've traveled the world by motorcycle, but it's always been as the guy in charge of a group of paying clients. I've led groups through Africa and Europe, as well as North and South America, but the inherent problem with tours is that you're always on a schedule. Tour leaders are also responsible for client safety and satisfaction, and frankly, there's never enough time to fully absorb the beauty or the culture of the places you're passing through.

Over the years, RawHyde has trained thousands of riders, and within those thousands I've met a lot of wonderful people. Among them are a few with whom I've become good friends, and it was from this select group that I began assembling the team you'll see on the pages of this book.

As for the name, well . . . all great journeys need a fitting title, right? Expedition 65 comes from the fact that Cartagena, Colombia, is 10 degrees north of the equator, and Ushuaia, Argentina, is 55 degrees south—totaling sixty-five degrees of latitude in the journey to the "end of the world."

As the owner of a very small company, it's impossible for me to take two and a half months away from the business without doing something that generates interest in our core mission. E-65 is a great story in and of itself, and I sincerely hope that you (the reader) find inspiration within these pages to go off and have your own grand adventure.

—Jim Hyde
Organizer, Expedition 65
Founder and Owner, RawHyde Adventures

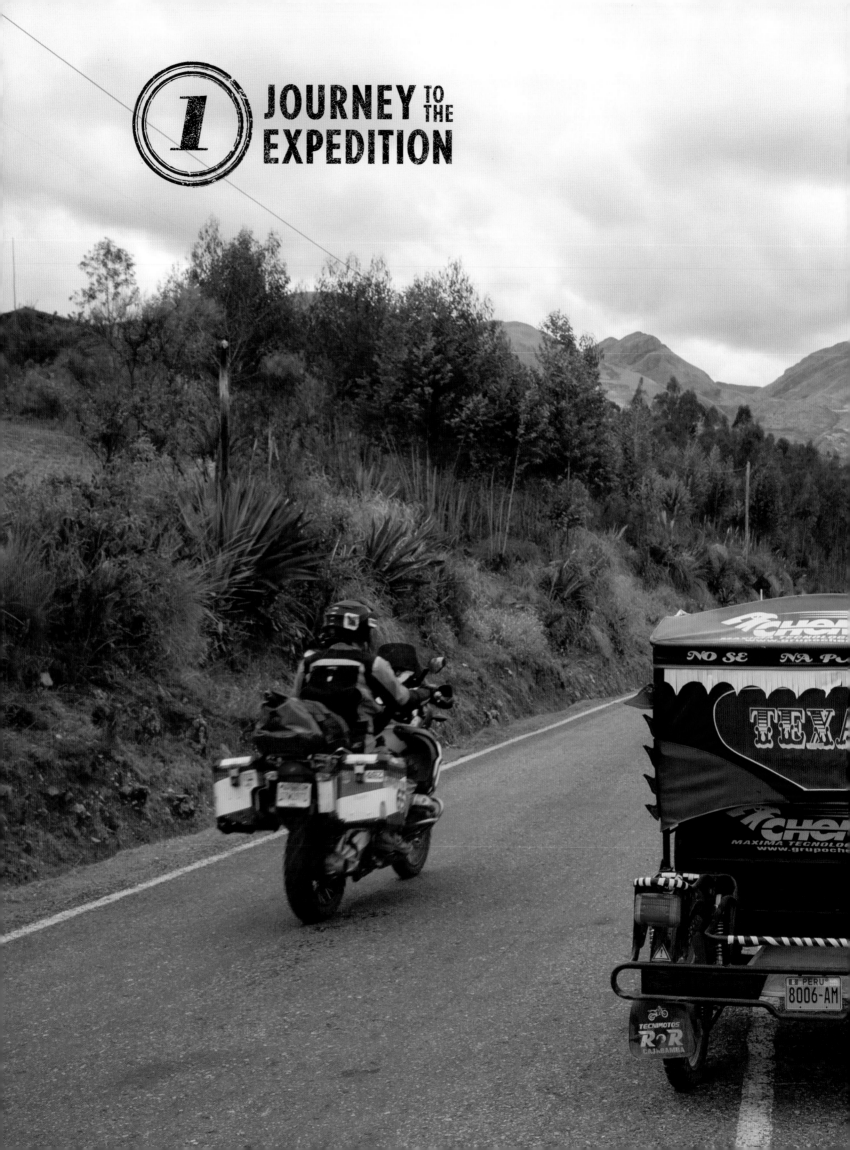

1 JOURNEY TO THE EXPEDITION

BIENVENIDOS
A
SHITABAMBA
PEDACITO DE CIELO
TIERRA DE
TRIUNFADORES
TECNIMOTOS
R&R
CAJABAMBA

The right gear is crucial
on a trip like this.
Thankfully, the whiskey
we'd packed made it
through customs!

INTO THE UNKNOWN

An expedition is serious business, especially when the destination is more than 10,000 miles from the starting point and meanders through six developing nations. The routing alone demands a lot of intense planning, and a careful inventory of specialized equipment to get you to the finish. Putting together the logistical side of Expedition 65 was a major undertaking that required a year and a half just to lay out! Equipping for the journey required the purchase of a custom 4X4 support van along with a military-grade trailer to keep the expedition's equipment secure and protected from the elements. Since the expedition would spend long amounts of time away from "civilization," we needed a kitchen, a water supply, water heaters, fuel reserves and safe storage, as well as generators and inverters to provide charging stations for the multitude of electronic devices we'd be juicing up daily.

Think about it—outfitting 15 guys with equipment that would keep them comfortable, safe, and functional in environments that could vary from a humid 100 degrees in the jungles of Colombia, to freezing temperatures at elevations of nearly 17,000 feet in Perú and Bolivia, to snow- and ice-covered trails in the lower latitudes of Patagonia.

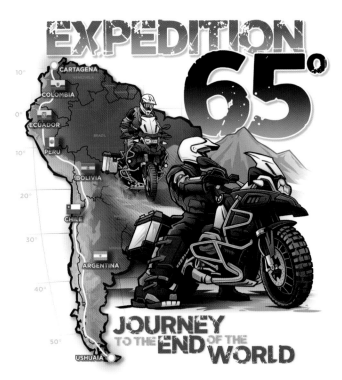

EXPEDITION 65°

JOURNEY TO THE END OF THE WORLD

13

THE BIKES / ACCESORIES

We used stock BMW R 1200 GS Adventure motorcycles on our journey, but of course there's always the question of equipping each machine for your own specific needs.

When it comes to prepping a motorcycle for a long trip like E-65, many of the final decisions boil down to preference rather than necessity: Do you want hard luggage or soft? Extra lighting or not? And there are probably a hundred more things to consider, but each new element also adds weight and possible "consequences," and frankly, I just like to keep it simple. For me, less stuff means less maintenance and hassle on the road.

I don't like to tinker with the actual mechanics of the machine either, preferring to leave it stock simply because I believe that's the most reliable configuration. Some items, however, are prime candidates for an upgrade, especially for a punishing trip like this. Here's my personal, highly subjective list:

1. Skid plate: Only because the stock piece provided by the manufacturer is there more to deflect "road debris" than grapefruit-sized rocks, and believe me, I heard many big stones bounce off the Black Dog Cycle Works plate I chose for the trip. It did its job well.

2. Lighting: This is important primarily for night driving in areas without street lights. To also provide increased visibility during the day, I chose the blindingly bright Clearwater Erica 6000 lumen LED lights. LEDs have made amazing strides in recent years as auxiliary lights and have supplanted HIDs, which had been the standard. More reliable and robust, and sipping energy at only 60 watts per light, the Ericas made my night driving infinitely safer by illuminating hazards at a much greater distance than the stock lighting ever could.

3. Luggage: Wow, such a polarizing topic. Hard or soft bags? I'm a fan of hard-sided aluminum luggage for one simple reason—it is lockable, and so is generally theft- proof. I've always joked that anyone with a razor can own your stuff if you have soft panniers, but the great benefit of soft luggage is that it's compressible, so your stuff won't rattle around (aluminum panniers allow hard bits to roll around somewhat). Soft luggage can typically be cinched up pretty tightly to minimize movement, but you can't lock textile saddlebags, and since I always carry a satellite phone and other pricy gizmos, I prefer aluminum. That, plus my good friend Al Jesse at Jesse Luggage Systems happens to make the finest panniers on the market (in my opinion). Naturally, his are my personal favorite.

4. Seats: Your saddle can make a real difference on a long ride. With a custom seat you can change your ride height, making it easier to get your feet on the ground—and it can also make your ride much more comfortable. Placing differing densities of foam in various places can also alter the whole "feel" of the seat. I worked with Rocky Mayer of Bill Mayer Saddles to work up a custom enduro-style seat for my 2016 BMW GSA, and I loved it for all 10,734 miles of the trip.

5. Electronics: That includes GPS, a communications system and satellite "text devices." There's simply no question that you need a GPS and some form of satellite communications for a trip like Expedition 65; I usually ride with two GPS systems, each showing different information. (I like having a spare in case one fails, as happened to me on this trip.) Equally important is the ability to communicate in the event of an accident or unexpected delay. I personally carry an Iridium satellite phone as well as a Delorme InReach satellite texting device. Both are satellite based—one being purely a telephone (the Iridium), while the inReach acts like a bridge between my cell phone and the satellites in orbit. The inReach is a super-cool device that pairs with your iPhone and allows you to text up to 160 characters at a time. As with cell phones, it offers various calling plans with certain levels of usage and prices, but it's a fabulous tool for the adventure rider. Don't leave home without one.

THE VAN AND TRAILER

Our support van was essentially a rolling warehouse. The 2016 long-wheelbase Ford Transit was converted to 4X4 drive by the Quigley Motor Company of Manchester, Pennsylvania. Quigley is the only company Ford authorizes to do such conversions of the Transit, and they have been working on them for more than 50 years. Although we'd have preferred a diesel, we went with a 3.5-liter gas EcoBoost motor because of the scarcity of low-sulphur diesel in the areas we'd be traveling. The van would also serve as the place where all the team's luggage, camping gear, and spares would be kept.

Other than the 4X4 conversion, the vehicle was kept mostly stock with the exception of an Aluminess custom winch bumper and a Warn 12,000 lb. winch to help extract us from the occasional mud bog or ditch.

The van also contains two ARB Fridge Freezers along with our first aid kit, air compressors, and a lot of other minor but necessary bits and pieces.

Our support trailer was truly a unique piece of engineering. Built by Schutt Industries of Clintonville, Wisconsin, it was the electronic nerve center of the trip, in addition to serving as kitchen, shower, fuel depot, and storage facility. The stout, "expedition grade" trailer is called the XVENTURE, and is based on a chassis that Schutt usually sells to the US military. The Schutt team worked closely with us to create an electrical system that would accommodate the three to four devices per person that'd need to be charged on a daily basis. The trailer contains nearly 70 USB charging points, as well as a 7000 watt Cummins generator to provide all that power.

THE GEOGRAPHY

Not only is it the fourth-largest continent, but South America can also lay claim to having some of the most extreme geographic variations and climates, including the world's longest mountain system (the Andes) and the world's largest river by volume (the Amazon). Geographically, South America forms the southern portion of the American landmass south and east of the Panama–Colombia border.

For Expedition 65, we set out to cross 65 degrees of latitude in 65 days, covering approximately 10,000 miles. We'd leave Cartagena, Colombia, at 10 degrees N, and aim for Ushuaia, Argentina—55 degrees south of the equator. Our route would roll from north to south down the spine of the Andes, occasionally zigzagging to points east before crossing the world's largest salt flat, the glaciers of

Known around the world as the Bolivian "Death Road," Yungas Road has been converted from a one-and-only, single-lane, scary-as-hell, two-way thoroughfare into a tourist trap with absolutely zero consideration for safety. You will no longer find truck traffic on this path, but you will be sharing it with other motorcycle riders and throngs of mountain bikers. It's thrilling as hell!

Patagonia, and then crossing the finish line in Tierra del Fuego at the world's end.

Ferdinand Magellan was the first European to poke around in this region while he was sailing to the East Indies on a Spanish expedition. Our idea was a bit simpler: 15 gentlemen of five nationalities, piloting 15 BMWs, with two guitars, one van, one trailer, one 8Kw generator, one driver, and one cook, would ride 10,000 miles through six countries with 13 international border crossings. We'd go from sea level in Colombia, through a few 15,000-foot passes in the Andes Mountains, and back down to sea level at our last stop in Ushuaia, Argentina.

Gentlemen, start your engines. Next stop—Cartagena.

2

COLOMBIA

Our bikes arrived in a container from Miami on schedule, and we spent the rest of the day extracting the bikes, van, and assorted gear from Colombian customs.

While awaiting entry paperwork in Cartagena, we entertained the Valley Group office with song and laughter.

OFFICIALLY ON THE ROAD

Yesterday, we spent about six hours extracting 15 bikes, one truck, one trailer, and an unconscionable amount of other stuff from the hands of Colombian Customs in the port of Cartagena. Usually this takes days, but it went way more quickly thanks to an enthusiastic local motorcyclist and his amazing staff at Valley Group. We are forever in debt to Victor Sierra and his team for their energy and patience in getting us on the road and for making all the pieces work.

For one thing, my bike fired up the first time, plus the two bottles of whiskey I'd stashed had not been commandeered by US or Colombia Customs. We got out of there in fairly good time and were soon creeping through the manic rush hour traffic of Cartagena.

At our staging area, the BMWs were soon sorted and the luggage secured. After one more day of reorganizing our crap and adding the team colors to our bikes via plastic wraps, we were now ready to head south in search of the heart—and the edge—of South America.

Landscapes do not get this green without loads of rain. Unfortunately for us, the first hours of the tour were very wet ones.

DAY 1
CROSSING COLOMBIA
Climate Is What You Expect—Weather Is What You Get

The first day out of Cartagena was intended to be a gentle break-in period; a cruise down to the beach and then an easy ride to camp at a ranch in Monter´Ia. Well, it didn't quite work out that way when a huge tropical thunderstorm followed us across 12 MILES of dirt beach road, turning it into a slippery, sloppy mess, with water crossings galore. At one point the instant rivers became too big for us to ford, and we had to pull over to wait for them to subside.

The locals didn't seem to mind, though, and we noticed one farmer on his mule having an easier time with the mud

than our BMWs were. But there was no mule option for us, and even for me—a lad brought up in England—this weather really was miserable.

Our destination that evening was a ranch in Montería famous for its prize Brahman bulls, whom we got to meet the next morning. These massive but docile creatures are pretty well pampered, and very used to being paraded around and shown in public—and as if to prove their star status, they had moves and poses ready for their moment with our cameras.

23

Colombia's climate isn't always welcoming. Lots of rainfall quickly turned our route into a giant mud-bath.

Unique experiences started on our very first night, at a private ranch in Montería. These prize-winning Brahma bulls are the pride of the entire region.

The town of Puerto Valdivia is known
for its proximity to a natural spring, so
our team engaged in some spiritual
(and motorcycle) cleansing.

DAY 2
BAPTISM ON THE RÍO CAUCA
Conversion and Spiritual Cleansing

Some days you ask, "How did this happen?" Then you realize that everything happens for a reason.

Leaving Montería, we all had bikes that were covered in hardened mud from the day before. Earlier, we had decided to split into smaller groups to avoid the logistics and time-wasting issues of the very large group—it takes a long while to fuel 15 bikes at a time.

As we tracked along the muddy, flooded Río Cauca, we could see the beginning of the Cordillera Occidental looming up through our windshields; this range represents the very northern tip of one of the three fingers of the Andes that push up through Colombia, and end, exhausted, in Venezuela and the Caribbean. In this valley, the good people of Puerto Valdivia have been given a bountiful resource with which to make a living—the natural spring that flows out of the mountains and into the Río Cauca. There are now all sorts of car and truck wash businesses along the road, ready to make every vehicle that passes by sparkling clean. Each one advertises their services with high-pressure jets of water

(presumably spring-fed) blasting into the air along the roadside.

We were not blind to the obvious: our very real needs had met a perfect solution here, so we parked the five bikes and stood back to watch as they were scrubbed and hosed down. The formerly crusty Beemers were soon immaculate and, as a bonus, we no longer had mud on our suits/ either.

One of our team, however, took this a little more seriously than you might expect. I present to you Evan Firstman—a rider who had decided this would not just be a simple task of motorcycle cleaning, but an opportunity to be spiritually cleansed. And it seems he wanted all of us to be similarly converted by the cascades of flowing water.

Then—soaking wet after doing this nutty thing—Brother Firstman decides to give a lecture on the importance of common-sense motorcycle maintenance, for future viewers of the movie of this trip.

Absurd. And perfect.

COLOMBIA

Medellín native Fernando Botero's plump statues can be seen at a lovely park in the city center, where his work is accessible to all.

DAY 3
MEDELLÍN—THE CITY OF ETERNAL SPRING

We escaped the heat and humidity of the tropical Caribbean by heading south into Medellín, a bustling city wedged in a narrow valley between the Western and Central Cordillera of the Andes, sitting at a more pleasant altitude of 5,000 feet. The weather is Goldilocks beautiful: not too cold, not too hot, but just right, all year round.

Medellín was settled late by the Spanish—simply because it's tough to get here. The earliest settlers were Jews escaping the Inquisition that was headquartered in Cartagena at the time. Unlike the rest of Spanish South America, which depended massively on imported slavery, these new settlers set up haciendas that they worked themselves. That streak of independence survives to this day, and Medellín is now a modern city with real infrastructure and a competent government, along with tons of local pride.

Its recent history, however, has been stained by the violence of the drug cartels. At one point, the traffickers had amassed so much wealth, they started to propose local public works investments and new political parties in Medellín. That didn't go down too well with the government, and the Colombian and US militaries pursued the infamous drug boss Pablo Escobar to his bloody assassination on a Medellín rooftop in 1993.

Now the city is one of the safest in the world, as well as a fashion, industry, and party capital. There are even Pablo Escobar–themed tour operations.

That's not to say that the drug business has gone away completely. The communist rebel army in the jungle (FARC) has taken over where the cartels left off. There is some hope however: in late 2016, the Colombian government signed a deal with the FARC to end the violence that has engulfed the country for more than five decades, with Congress ratifying the peace agreement soon thereafter. Time will tell if it holds.

In the face of all these troubles, the people here have a saying: *los buenos somos más*, or "We good guys outnumber the bad guys."

One of those good guys, and a favorite son of Medellín, is the artist Fernando Botero, whose work is commemorated with a lovely park in the center of the city, featuring a large number of his bronze art pieces. You could call them Rubenesque, but I think Botero deserves to be acknowledged for his own style. They're so irresistibly plump, you can see where onlookers have been tempted to touch the statues, which has lightened the metal's hue. Even my fellow rider Alfonse and I couldn't help doing the same thing. Call us vandals if you must; we prefer to think of ourselves as art connoisseurs.

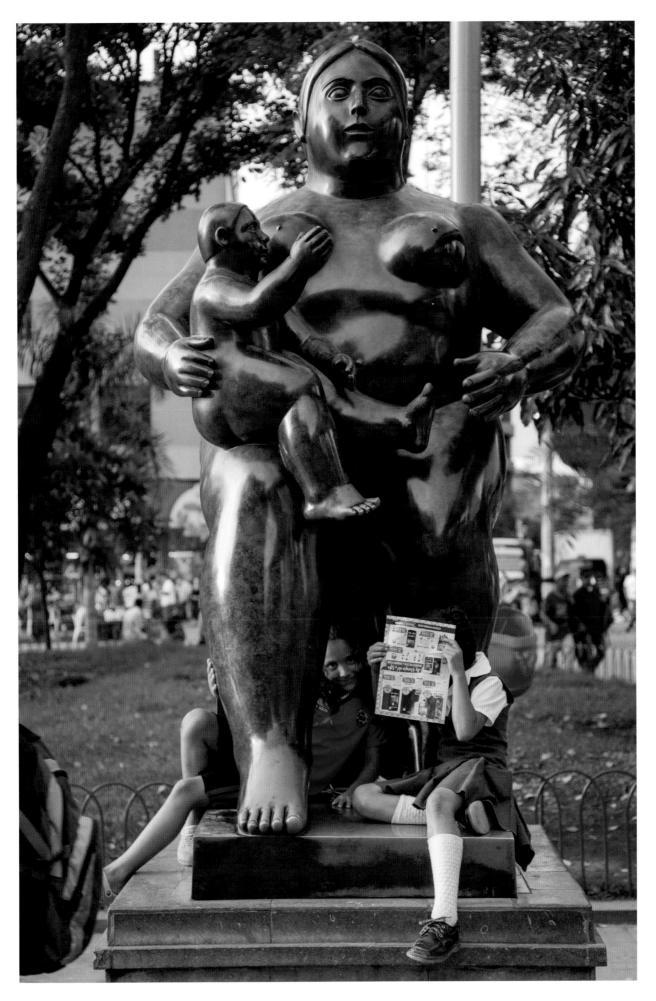

DAY 6
SUGAR CANE IN COLOMBIA

Threading between coffee plantations and fields of sugar cane are numerous fertile routes across the northern Colombian landscape near Armenia.

Visions of beauty surround you in Colombia, whether it's exquisitely hand-pulled lattes or verdant rolling hills.

Today we rode from Alcalá along the Valle del Cauca in the Zona Cafétera, which is the heart of the sugar and coffee industry in Colombia. In hours and hours of riding, we glimpsed nothing but sugarcane fields and coffee plantations. The climate here is such that sugarcane can grow year round and be harvested constantly. It is then transported to the processors in enormous fleets of tren cañero, or, "cane trains," that menace the roads in five-trailer configurations.

Sugar is an industry with its tentacles tightly wrapped around the political process in Colombia, but to my mind the setup is no different from one we have in the United States.

For example: the landowners in this area amassed more acreage and power during the La Violencia civil war from 1946 on, when politics exploded and the FARC took to the hills to fight. During a 10-year period, millions of people were forcibly removed from thousands of separate properties, to the point where now just one conglomerate owns the majority of the land in the valley. To further bolster demand, the sugar lobby has convinced the government to mandate that sugar ethanol be mixed with gasoline. How is that possible? Well, it seems the lobby has strong media connections and powerful ties to the state, has supported the last few presidents, and also helped much of the Colombian Congress get elected. Sound familiar? Replace "sugar" with "corn" and the scenario feels nearly identical to that in the States, with the corn lobby.

Perhaps there is one important difference. Maybe in the United States we can claim to have countervailing forces that help prevent this level of wholesale government influence by business interests. We have a strong and independent press that is focused on revealing corruption and holding officials and companies to high standards of ethics and legal compliance. We . . . Oh, never mind—the United States is just like Colombia.

Our group made the local kids grin when we showed up bearing new soccer balls, donated by Nike.

Even the village soccer coach in El Estrello wanted to get in on the action when he saw us roll up.

DAY 9
BIG BIKES IN SMALL PUEBLOS

Whenever a group of us shows up in a small town on our big bikes, we are invariably the center of interest.

There just aren't any large motorbikes in South America; anything above 150cc causes as much stir as if a Ferrari had rolled into town. Naturally, you have to field the inevitable questions, such as, *"¿Qué motor?"* to which one has to be able to reply (in Spanish), *"Mil doscientos"* (1200cc). When they ask, *"¿Qué velocidad?"* everyone gasps after you tell them *"Doscientos"* (200 kph). But if the topic turns to the price of the motorcycle, it's probably best to change the subject—the cost of a new BMW R 1200 GS in Colombia is four times the per capita GDP.

And if you show up with big bikes AND a few soccer balls (ours were donated by Nike for the trip), a crowd gathers instantly. On the ride from Popayán to Pasto, we pulled into El Estrello and found the local soccer pitch—a dirt patch set way back from the main road. Within minutes there was a pack of kids and their parents gathered around us, and when the town soccer coach heard about our appearance, he quickly turned up as well, his whistle hanging like a badge of office around his neck. We all had a great time kicking tires, as well as kicking the ball.

34

3

ECUADOR

THE MIDDLE OF THE EARTH

Crossing international borders is always a complicated matter, and horrendous rain doesn't make the process any smoother.

We may have crossed into a strange new country, but as members of the wonderful brotherhood of worldwide adventure motorbike riders, we have some valuable benefits at our disposal. Perhaps the most rewarding of these is the hospitality extended by the local riders. In Ecuador, we were hosted by the Brosters Group—the country's BMW riders club, based in Quito. These generous guys opened their arms and decided to show us all that Ecuador has to offer, even while providing hands-on support for our bikes in country.

Our deep dive into the Ecuadorean experience began north of Quito, at Laguna de Yahuarcocha (Lake of Blood) near Ibarra. In 1487, after defeating the Caranquis, the Inca king Huayna Capac ordered that all males over 12 years old be killed. When 30,000 bodies were then dumped into the lake, it turned red with their blood (or so the story goes). Today the lake is a much more tranquil place, with a pleasant picnic and recreation area that includes, of all things, Ecuador's only road circuit.

That's right: a race track. Family members of one of the Brosters led the effort to build this track in the 1960s, and we were fortunate enough to be granted full access to it for a couple of hours. Sure—let's put 15 guys riding fully loaded, knobby-tire-equipped BMW R 1200 GS bikes on a track—what could possibly go wrong? I know what you're thinking, but actually, every rider and his too-heavy rig managed to sail through the course unscathed, and we all had an absolute blast tearing around the fast, 2.3-mile Autódromo Internacional José Tobar on our adventure machines.

Of course the Brosters were keen to show us a slice of the local culture too, so we pushed onward to Otavalo in the Imbabura Province, which holds Ecuador's most important craft market. The Otavaleños have been masters of weaving textiles (usually wool) for centuries, and both the Incas and Spanish exploited these indigenous craftspeople and their unique skills. Although their quality of life has improved thanks to growing tourism at their famous open-air Saturday market, Otavaleños and other indigenous Ecuadorians might still be considered near the bottom of the country's social and economic ladder. In this case we are happy to spend our tourist dollars, as they really can make a difference.

Membership in Ecuador's BMW club has its privileges, including access to a private racetrack! Thanks to The Brosters we got the chance to skim a few miles off our knobbies before entering Quito.

The "other" museum built to mark the equator is called the Intiñan Solar Museum, a private attraction that is actually a bit closer to the true line.

Intrepid explorers can pose on the alleged equatorial line at the monument built to celebrate the French Geodesic Mission of the early 18th century, which proved that the earth bulged at the equator.

DAY 10
A SHORT HISTORY OF THE EQUATOR

No discussion of Ecuador is complete without a brief primer on the form of our planet. The ancient Greeks started the ball rolling on the process of understanding the earth's shape; Pythagoras himself first suggested that it could be a ball in space, and later, Eratosthenes designed a method for calculating the size of that ball in space by measuring arcs on a meridian and the angles to the sun. Hipparchus then designed the 360-degree grids of latitude and longitude for the ball in space. All this was established before 100 BC, no less.

The magnetic compass wouldn't come to Europe until around the 12th century, but its existence finally allowed for reliable long-distance navigation. Well, somewhat reliable; Christopher Columbus got his directions horribly wrong back in 1492, but the Spanish didn't mind because he'd found them rich new lands. In fact, Columbus's error did point out that the

world was bigger than previously assumed, and that, in turn, stimulated the birth of a new science—geodesy, the study of the exact size and shape of the Earth.

By the early 18th century, the debate had morphed into another France versus England spat—was Isaac Newton right that gravitational effects would cause the rotating globe to bulge at the equator, or was René Descartes right that particles streaming from the sun carry all the planets and cause the planet to be slim-waisted? A lot of national pride was at stake, so in the 1730s the French Academy of Sciences sent teams of scientists to Lapland and South America to measure their arcs and figure this global-shape thing out once and for all.

It is hard today to imagine how arduous it must have been to travel from France to the west coast of South America, and from there, hop onto the terrifying

mule train to Quito, whose path ran over rope bridges and along sheer cliffs. The researchers' work stretched over several years, and infighting took its toll on the delegation. Only five out of the original nine members made it back to France, but in the end (spoiler alert!), Newton was proved right.

Indeed, Earth has a bulging waistline.

Some 15 miles north of Quito is the Monument to the Equator, built around 1980 to celebrate that first French Geodesic Mission. In the years since its completion,

however, subsequent studies have determined that the line of the equator—latitude 0—is actually 250 meters from where the building stands. Despite that fact, hordes of tourists continue to snap photos of the line in the wrong location, but even with that caveat, you have to admit that the original geodesic mission had an astonishing level of accuracy given the technology available in 1736.

On a final note, Ecuador got its name when Finnish scientists in the 1800s declared it to be the prime place on Earth to measure the equator's bulge. Class dismissed.

In the eastern foothills near Chimborazo, our path rolls through lush green valleys and into a town named for the place where the water flows, Baños.

ECUADOR HIGHLANDS—CLOSEST TO HEAVEN

Today our gracious motorcycling hosts, the Brosters, led us from Quito to Baños the long way around—by circling the volcano Chimborazo on dirt roads. That was all fine by us, for we got to experience a true sense of the landscape, of the indigenous people, and of the real Ecuador.

About Chimborazo: When the German explorer Alexander von Humboldt and his French assistant, Aimé Bonpland, climbed and surveyed the 20,565-foot high mountain in 1802, it was thought to be the highest in the world. It is, in fact, the farthest point as measured from the center of the earth, due to the aforementioned bulging waistline of our planet. In Ecuador, though, they say it more poetically: this is the piece of the world closest to heaven.

Here, in the Avenue of Volcanoes in northern Ecuador from Quito to Cuenca, running between the two cordilleras of the Andes, there are seven peaks over 17,000 feet, and it's said that they ALL are farther from the center of the earth than Mount Everest. But more recently we have adopted mean sea level (MSL) as a datum for measuring altitude because altitude

46

Downtown or down-range, curious locals show up
every time we stop to take photographs.

from sea level takes into account what humans care about most—levels of oxygen.

One of the powerful effects of these massive volcanoes is that they mess with the climate. On the west side of the cones lies arid desert, while on the rainy east side, there are huge tracts of lush, green cattle ranches. We bumped into indigenous people living very different lives on either side.

On the dry side—a woman coming back from shopping carrying her purchases on a mule many miles from anywhere, and a group of farmers tending sheep and llamas on land that can barely support plant life. On the wet side—horsemen decked out in gaucho gear that probably hasn't changed in centuries, roping calves at a weekend rodeo. We stopped and took photos and joined a number of spectators who were watching the universally shit-faced horsemen (drunk on local moonshine) enter the ring to try and rope calves.

As we got back on the bikes and rode past Chimborazo, it even SNOWED on us.

DAY 13
THEY CALL IT A RAIN FOREST FOR A REASON

The geography of South America is pretty simple if you think about it; the continent only has three parts. There's the Amazon, the Andes, and the Rest. All right, it might be a bit more complicated than that, since the Rest is made up of the drier parts of Brazil, plus the Pampas in Argentina, plus Patagonia. But still pretty simple.

For Expedition 65 we decided to essentially travel down the spine of the Andes, from the top of South America to the bottom, or, north to south. We would,

however, be zigzagging a bit and dropping into Amazonia a couple of times. On this day we opted to head east from Baños in Ecuador, and across South America's continental divide in the dramatic canyon along the Pastaza River, which is one of 1,100 tributaries that drain into the Amazon.

The weather we encountered on this stretch was absolutely foul—we battled heavy rain for hours as we made our way south through the rainforest and toward Cuenca. The rain went from acute to chronic

Were it not for the previous six hours of rain-soaked riding, we probably would have been more interested in checking out this waterfall across the street from the hotel in Baños.

but never stopped, and all the rivers in view were in full flow, bubbling over rocks and ripping up sediment in a brown swirling soup. The rain that didn't expend its energy soaking us to the bone would shortly end up in this river, then the Amazon, and eventually spill out into the Atlantic Ocean about 5,000 miles downstream.

The first person to make this same journey was Francisco de Orellana, in 1541. He set off in search of food for Pizarro's marauding conquistadors but got mesmerized by the potential of what he saw, and then, as they all did,

took off to seek out the mythic golden city of El Dorado, thinking it was in the nearby jungle. A few months later his party was attacked by an indigenous group that claimed a female god as their leader. He was so convinced his party was being ambushed by women, he named the river after the mythical women warriors of ancient Greece— the Amazons. After a hard eight months in the jungle, he arrived at the Atlantic, thus becoming the first European to travel the length of the Amazon. Nobody else would manage to do this again for a hundred years.

ECUADOR

4 PERÚ

A row of "little reed horses" stacked up right next to a more modern conveyance— the iron horse.

DAY 17

CABALLITOS DE TOTORA, OR "LITTLE REED HORSES"

Caballito is Spanish for "seahorse," and *Caballitos de totora* are the reed fishing boats ridden like horses into the water by fishermen in Pimentel—a small rustic village on the coast by Chiclayo, Perú. Their wave-riding technique predates any European contact, though I'd guess the addition of styrofoam in the stern of each vessel probably came later. I talked to one fisherman who told me that these unique boats can land anything from anchovies to shark.

We had ended up in Pimentel after an ugly haul away from the border: 400 miles down the *Panamericana* highway in a straight, windy, hot, and boring grind across the coastal desert. The "fast group" had hit upon a funky camp that was a cross between the

Whole Earth Catalog and Burning Man, and they gave us a vague call to come "sleep on the beach." Upon arrival, some of us decided that our tents were a safer and more flea-free environment than the wacky pyramid-shaped bamboo structures we found scattered around the campgrounds. If Perú has a spring break equivalent, I bet it'll be happening here.

Sleeping arrangements notwithstanding, what I found most astonishing was the fact that our camp host in this esoteric encampment somehow managed to produce the best meal we'd had so far—a couple of fresh fish cooked two different ways, along with a succulent chicken and a tasty salad, and perhaps most importantly, BEER.

This slightly shabby camping spot on the Perúvian shore featured pyramids, fire pits, and a fantastic meal for our tired group.

Fully suited up and guiding our huge machines along the sand, we earned plenty of inquisitive stares from the beach-bound youngsters near Pimentel.

In a small concrete plaza, our parade of First World wanderers crashed into the local tribes of Angasmarca with a glorious explosion of color and sound.

DAY 20
THE RÍO TABLACHACA VALLEY
And the Most Dangerous Road I've Ridden

Riding in the Andes is breathtaking, electrifying, and completely terrifying. Leaving Pallasca, we dropped 7,000 feet down to the Río Tablachaca on roads that have absolutely zero room for error—one slip and there's only the abyss to greet you.

This entire road was paved once upon a time, but now large sections have been eroded away by landslides or earthquakes and have only been crudely patched up. Even on sections that are still intact, truck and bus traffic has ripped every hairpin bend into potholes, and long stretches have mounds of pebbles and scree piled up in the center. That may be no problem for trucks, but it's a nightmare for motorbikes. The pucker factor is off the scale when you ride here.

Almost as dangerous are the views. Huge, colorful panoramas appear around every bend, but you'd better stop if you want to enjoy them; you simply cannot look at the road and the scenery at the same time. But I couldn't help myself. In the distance, I spot fellow riders Evan and Chris dropping down one section of hairpins; Alfonse and Bill pausing before heading for the traverse farther down the canyon; Evan riding the edge of the canyon on a road that's barely carved out of the vertical cliff; A fellow rider coming out of a tunnel in the lower section of the road. Every twist and turn is surreal. And when I do stop and expand my perspective, it's even more amazing to realize there are people all around who manage to eke out a living by farming this hostile landscape.

Living off the land in any way possible, these folks tend to a placer mine along the Río Tablachaca, looking for elusive gold pebbles.

DAY 21
LA POLICÍA LATINOAMERICANA

The police forces in Latin America do not have a very good reputation for honesty. They are rarely trusted by the citizenry, they're mostly underpaid, and they often resort to creative ways to increase their compensation, usually by taking a bite out of locals and tourists alike.

For some reason, our experience so far in South America has been quite the opposite. Maybe it's because we are big men traveling in packs on large, garishly decorated bikes, and we always attract a crowd. Frankly, we're not the perfect marks for petty graft; it would be very difficult to pick on us singly, or even to privately extract a bribe.

Or maybe I'm just naive, because I haven't seen even a hint of this. Our every interaction to date has been with officers who have behaved politely and professionally. The police in Cartagena helped direct our night ride in the Plaza Grande, highway patrol cars often wave us over double yellow lines at highly illegal speeds, and the local patrolman is always the one to ask us for a photograph. Traffic police have broken away from checking truck paperwork to chat us up, while motorcycle cops have saluted, and small-town constables have more than once organized crowd control to allow us safe passage.

Today a few of us stopped in a dusty town just off the Pan-American Highway north of Lima for fuel and snacks. We left our bikes in the shade of the gas station awning and went into the little store for sugary goodies. After a few minutes, one of the local police trucks pulled up and the senior officer approached, asking about our trip, shaking our hands, and then pointing out that this was one of the highest-crime neighborhoods in Perú. If our bikes and helmets were not nailed down, he said, they could disappear in a flash. The store clerk confirmed that recently two armed guys had stolen motorbikes from this very station. We got the hint and stood up to leave, but the officer wouldn't have it. "No, please finish your drinks. My colleague and I will guard your bikes," he insisted. They then parked next to the bikes for as long as it took us to get dressed and ready, wished us *buen viaje*, and left.

My overall impression is that these officers were just as curious about our trip as everyone else, but they also wanted these crazy, high-profile foreigners to feel welcome, and to leave with a positive image of their country.

For that, officers, we thank you. Protect and Serve.

Traveling in South America inures you to a wide variety of accommodations. Flypaper is optional.

DEAR ABBY, HELP: I AM BECOMING AN ADVENTURE TOURISM SNOB

Over the last month I've traveled by motorbike along the Andes with a group of friends, starting in Cartagena, Colombia, passing through Ecuador, and now flopping in Cusco, Perú. We have stayed in condos, hotels and hostels, and camped on farms, by lakes, and under the tailings of a gold mine. Our beds have cost anywhere from $3 to hundreds of dollars per night. One night we stayed at a beach compound that could have passed for a refugee camp. Our food has varied from haute cuisine to simple, local grilled foods to excellent chicken soup—with the feet still floating in it.

We have ridden on every kind of road, from first-class motorways to dodgy, dangerous hills to deep water and mud, to dirt roads that felt like they were made of pebbles mixed with talcum powder.

We have been to towns and villages that have rarely, if ever, seen strangers passing through, and we have been welcomed with complete warmth and generosity everywhere we wandered.

Today, though, I am in an upscale hotel in Cusco for a couple of days to regroup and get refreshed for the rigors to come in Bolivia, the Altiplano, and the Atacama Desert. The hotel is filled with earnest westerners with the right gear and the right cameras, about to enjoy the Valley of the Incas and Machu Picchu. The hotel even offers an option to add oxygen to the air in your room, in addition to guide and spa services.

This is the first time in a month that I have felt like a tourist.

At the truly world-class breakfast buffet this morning, a lady was complaining that she couldn't find her favorite cheese, and that the toaster wasn't as quick as the one at home. I felt like grabbing her and saying, "Ferfucksake, woman, I ate in a restaurant last week that had flypaper hanging over the table. And Señor ´Alvarez put us up in his guest room for $3. Stop bothering these people!"

I feel angry and alien. Do I need help?

WE HAD TERRORISTS BEFORE AL QUEDA

Every time a brown person with a name like Mohammed attacks someone, the American media swings into full hysteria and claims that our country faces an existential threat from Islamic terror. This is total nonsense; more people were killed in the United States last year by armed toddlers than by sworn terrorists. But fear makes for good headlines and drives ratings, and myths continue to be good for business and for politics alike.

We Euros have had terrorism in our midst for decades, of course. In my own lifetime, "The Troubles" in Northern Ireland spilled across Great Britain as Catholics and Protestants killed, tortured, and bombed. There was the Red Brigade, the Baader-Meinhof gang, and Basque separatists. All of them were left-wing armed groups trying to make themselves heard in an indifferent world, like little children lying on the floor holding their breath until they get dessert.

In Perú, the period of home-grown terror came from the Shining Path. This organization was founded in the 1960s by Abimael Guzmán, a philosophy professor at the university in Ayacucho. For a decade or so he found willing recruits in the impressionable students and the indigenous Quechua farmers being ignored by the government that, at the time, was a military dictatorship. Both groups thought the Shining Path would help them on the road to social justice and tackle the extreme economic inequalities and exploitation of people in the highlands.

When elections came in 1980, however, they turned into armed violence, with the destruction of private property, burning of ballot boxes, and assassinations being the immediate result. Despite the fact that Guzmán said, "The triumph of the revolution will cost a million lives," the government initially ignored all that violence. But every authority eventually flexes its muscles, so the feds finally snapped and overreacted, with the indigenous communities bearing the brunt from both sides. The Shining Path campaigned across the country, but their homeland was the Andean highlands, which they controlled for over a decade, until Guzmán was captured and sentenced to life in 1992.

In Ayacucho there is a small, dusty museum run by a group of Quechua women who lost family members to this insanity. Their organization was founded in 1983, long before the "civil war" came to an end. Their goal is to bring these crimes against their husbands, children, and fathers to the attention of a larger world.

A couple of us visited with and talked to the docent about her life. She told us she lost her father as a small child, and explained the evolution of the conflict and the wrongs still un-righted. She was particularly emotional when telling us that many of Guzmán's lieutenants were being released at the end of their jail terms and returning to join the remaining 500 or so Shining Path members in the Amazon part of Perú, to traffic cocaine.

Overall, 69,000 Perúvians suffered violent deaths from murder, torture, and rape during this period, the majority of them the country's poorest citizens. But how do you show this in a museum? All they can do is reflect the media coverage of the time and include art projects that portray how those affected feel. The motto of the museum is "So this never happens again." Well, of course it can't—can it? I'm not so sure.

We still have politicians in our midst that rise to power by demonizing others, including one that's now the leader of the free world. They all blame other groups for our problems and promise to make that group go away. Pick your responsible party—the king, the Tsar, the capitalists, the bourgeoisie, the Jews, the "welfare queens," or the immigrants. Then cut off their heads, and your troubles are solved. We know that's not true, but, once again, it drives ratings and votes.

So I'm back to where I started. Beware of simple answers, selfish media, and angry citizens.

When it comes to law enforcement, Perú's government believes women are more efficient—and less corruptible— and make for better officers.

WOMEN ARE LESS CORRUPT THAN MEN

Females are less susceptible to bribes than males. At least that's what senior police officers in Perú believe. Drive anywhere in Perú and you will see the traffic at rush hour being directed by lovely young ladies on motorcycles, wearing crisp green uniforms, Ray-Bans, tan jodhpurs, and riding boots. Since 1998 these women have been at the vanguard of improving public perception of law enforcement, in a country known for rampant corruption. Male traffic cops have been assigned to desk jobs and the ladies have taken over, everywhere.

Today 11 percent of officers in the PNP (Perú's National Police) are women, but in the Lima traffic division, it's a staggering 93 percent. The police bosses are happy, "since female officers are more harsh at giving tickets, are strict and are difficult to bribe." When the program was first started, it seems a lot of taxi drivers were initially up in arms at the fact that they could no longer get away with a common transgression, reckless driving. A simple bribe would usually erase the violation, but not anymore.

The policy has spread across all of Perú with great success, but I cannot imagine the kind of lewd comments and disrespect that these women must encounter every day in a macho Latin country. Regardless, I surely do not plan to mess with them in any way while I am here.

PERÚ

Got milk? The author almost had a very close call with this doyenne of the dairy farm.

DAY 24
I MET THIS LADY AND IMMEDIATELY MADE A CONNECTION

There are many perils to watch for on Perú's roads—aggressive, lunatic drivers in barely maintained cars, deep culverts off narrow, twisty roads, invisibly deep and slippery rain channels, and tiny ladies in multiple frilly petticoats and felt hats herding sheep, with all the time in the world.

This last one was new to me.

Leaving Ayacucho on a very narrow and twisty road that connected all the small farms, I spied a line across the road. At the last minute I realized that it was actually a rope tethering a cow to a tree. The radius from the tree had allowed the cow to cross the road to find better grazing and the rope was strung across my

right of way. Before I could react, it whipped under my front wheel, then jammed into the sump guard. I was stunned, and the cow was none too pleased to be yanked rudely off her favorite grass and dragged down the road.

I was worried that she could have easily pulled the rope tight and flipped the bike, but she just stood there passively while another rider ran over to extract the rope. She did evacuate her bowels in front of us, of course; a real treat. I'm not sure if this was from fear or just to show us what she thought about her mistreatment, I'm just glad she hadn't pulled the line tighter, or this story may have had a less humorous ending.

During our rest days in Cusco, friends of RawHyde Adventures joined us to visit the Incan site of Machu Picchu. Rider Evan Firstman and his buddy Owen (pictured) made the four-hour train ride to the ruins a ton more fun.

DAY 27
IF YOU'RE A TOURIST, BE A TOURIST

A few lovely days off in Cusco, at the center of the Valley of the Incas, had us booking a trip via boring bus / twisty train / scary bus to get to Machu Picchu, the 15th-century former country retreat of the Inca kings. Cusco really is a beautiful city that has retained enough from its various historical periods to interest any curious wandering tourist. But the real payoff was Machu Picchu, which really is breathtaking (literally, if you started to rush around the stone ruins at their 8,000 feet elevation), especially under glowering rain clouds.

PERÚ

73

cafe mayu
espresso coffee togo
LOCAL CRAFT BEER
SERVED HERE
WI FI

Feeding the free-range llamas in Machu Picchu is a no-no. But nowhere is it written that they can't steal what we're eating.

If you're a tourist, be a tourist and collect your friends together for an epic photo. Moments like these happen but once in a lifetime.

THE PERÚ FARMERS' UNION MEETING

As we left Laguna Pacucha and headed to Cusco, we came across a gathering at the side of the road. I managed to talk to a couple of the people turning up and learned that it was a regular meeting of the farmers' union.

The men were ranged on bleachers dug from sod around a square meeting place surrounded by their fields at 12,000 feet elevation, and the women in open toe sandals stayed close at hand to share what was going on and look after the children, and perhaps to check how much money the men were supposed to be bringing home. In the middle a few men were addressing a crowd that was paying very close attention.

It would have been fascinating to get closer and listen in, but this party was definitely invitation only and my Quechua is a little rusty anyway. I am sure they were talking about the usual farmer stuff, like market prices and the weather, but there also seem to be two big themes animating indigenous politics in these parts.

First is the threat to traditional farming. The people here have been managing to farm this hostile environment for a millennium, and they've learned a few things. Traditional methods involve a high degree of seed sharing and knowledge, and the campesino farmers have become the main conservers of genetic diversity, native crops, and their wild relatives. This is threatened by big agricultural concerns that would love to be able to deliver genetically modified seeds and expensive custom fertilizers and pesticides. If the big companies have their way, the farmer would then own the seeds the same way we own software; we have a license to use it, but we can't copy it. That would be the end of any kind of seed preservation

People in this hostile environment have learned to farm the land and thrive upon it for ages.

and sharing and a blow to biodiversity—and the Andean Quechua, so far, are having none of it.

Second, these people may be poor but they have power; Perú is a democracy, and these farmers vote. In 2001, Alejandro Toledo became the first president from an indigenous Quechua family, and he held his inauguration at Machu Picchu instead of the capital, Lima. In 2011 Perú passed a law "Protecting the Collective Knowledge of Indigenous Peoples," that requires prior informed consent from communities before accessing traditional knowledge,

and is supposed to enforce sharing of benefits. The right to save and use seeds is also recognized in national law.

So far it seems that the "sharing of benefits" part of the equation hasn't worked out too well; trickle-down economics is as big a hoax in Perú as it is in the United States But the good news is that the poorest of the poor have a voice in these debates. In our corporatized US Congress, I cannot imagine the interests of indigenous peoples or poor farmers being given this much attention in the face of Big Ag business lobbying.

PERÚ

Our condor-spotting trip to Colca Canyon eventually turned into a photo contest. Everybody won this time.

DAY 30
COLCA CANYON CONDORS

If you want to see real Andean Condors then you must go to Colca Canyon in southern Perú. The ride along the edge of the canyon from Chivay is a spectacular reason alone to make the trip. The locals claim that Colca Canyon is the world's deepest, but Perú's own tourist organization says that honor belongs to Cotahuasi Canyon just west of Colca, while the Chinese say they have the deepest at Yarlung Tsangpo in Tibet. It seems to depend on how you measure it, but Colca and the various active volcanoes surrounding it are breathtaking enough. Despite its 10,000-foot depth, the canyon is intensively farmed,

with astonishing terraces carved along every feasible slope, and handmade walls that must have been built over many centuries.

The main condor hangout is a location where the canyon narrows and the wind blows constantly. Condors can have wingspans of up to 10 feet and are jet black all over; we spotted one specimen who insisted on effortlessly strafing us. This one was smaller, fluffier, and grayer, so he was likely a youngster. These guys mate for life and can live to be 60 years old, and the so-called "Eternity Bird" is quite an impressive sight to see up close.

83

PERÚ

Woven into local mythology and folklore, the Andean condor is a national symbol in every country we rode through, and the sight of these majestic birds is truly awesome.

84

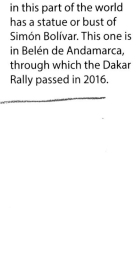
Regardless of population size, every town square in this part of the world has a statue or bust of Simón Bolívar. This one is in Belén de Andamarca, through which the Dakar Rally passed in 2016.

I'LL TAKE COUNTRIES NAMED FOR PEOPLE FOR *$400*, ALEX

There are three countries named after people in South America—one for Christopher Columbus (Colombia), and two for Simón Bolívar (Bolivia and the Bolivarian Republic of Venezuela).

Historical accounts naturally draw you to the stories of great people, and as we learn them, we develop a short list of our own heroes. They're usually complex characters who changed the world even while dealing with their own demons. Growing up in the UK, my history lessons focused on the people who put the greatness into Great Britain, and my own two obsessions have been Lawrence of Arabia and Winston Churchill.

But I think Simón Bolívar deserves to be on that list. His story is astonishing and complex, and the opportunity for one person to achieve what he did could only have happened in the early nineteenth century.

He was born into wealth and educated by his nurse, a family slave, and tutors. He traveled in Europe as a military cadet, witnessed the coronation of Napoleon at Notre Dame, and came home with a head full of ideas from the Enlightenment. He put his life and money into leading a military liberation of a continent from Spain at the age of 25, and was appointed president of Venezuela, Gran Colombia (present-day Colombia, Venezuela, Ecuador, and Panamá), Bolivia, and Perú. His first wife died, and he stayed true to his vow to marry nobody else, but had a voracious appetite for women. He also had one constant lover, Manuela Sáenz, who prevented an assassination attempt against him, and was such a close collaborator that he called her *"Libertadora del Libertador."* His dream of a politically unified continent fell apart under the pressure and greed of the Church and local oligarchs, who settled the borders of the current countries of South America. He died a broken man, unwilling to leave the countries he had liberated and ruled.

Our ride so far has passed through a few key places in Bolívar's story. We started in Cartagena where he died, passed through Ayacucho where the Spanish were finally defeated, and then rode to Cusco where a statue celebrates his lap of honor in 1825 through many of the cities that revered him.

One book that aptly describes his life is *The General in His Labyrinth*, by Gabriel García Márquez. It charts the last 30 days of his life, as he left Bogotá and his dreams behind, but could not bring himself to step on the boat at Cartagena to accept exile.

PERÚ

All kids are curious types, and this young body is loving the bird's-eye view of his village's homes relayed from tour leader Jim Hyde's remote drone.

DAY 31
WHATEVER FLOATS YOUR HOME

Today we visited the Uros Islands in Lake Titicaca, which straddles the border between Perú and Bolivia. There are now 87 islands, containing 4,600 inhabitants and three elementary schools—all floating on rafts of reed roots, covered with layers of reeds. At one point, we met five families that were all living on one island.

This island lifestyle started as a defensive strategy against the Inca, as in this configuration, the islands could be detached and moved. Unfortunately, the clever strategy did not stop the Uro people (who intermarried and merged with the Aymara) from being eventually conquered and enslaved by the Spanish. But it's an interesting story anyway, and today about half of the Uros' income comes from sharing their accounts and lives with tourists, while the other half comes from jobs they take on the "mainland," in Puno.

Known locally as "Rolls-Royce" ships, these sail-less reed boats are used to take tourists from island to island for a few extra cents .

The people of Uros, living on self-made reed islands floating on the world's highest lake, Lake Titicaca, attract tourists from the shores of Puno on an hourly basis.

The view from atop the lookout tower on one of the 87 floating islands of Uros.

BOLIVIA 5

Measuring 4,000 square miles, the Salar de Uyuni is the world's largest salt flat. Those distinctive hexagonal shapes are a function of the crystalline structure of the salt.

DAY 34
THE ONLY WAY IS UP

Traveling in South America means having to constantly adjust your perspective between the stunning natural beauty of the countryside and the choking poverty and pollution of the cities. The towns are overrun with farm animals, the cities crammed with construction, and the roads are packed with passenger vans shuttling people in all directions. To top it all off, buses and trucks with unmaintained diesel engines spew carcinogens in the form of vast, indiscriminate black clouds that seem to linger everywhere.

La Paz, Bolivia, is a perfect example. There is probably no city in the world more visually stunning than La Paz, which sits at 11,000 feet in a canyon protected from the Altiplano winds and the worst of the high-altitude weather. From the edge of a nearby cliff, the views of this urban center are amazing. Originally a small mining town when the Spanish showed up to

run the show in the 1500s, today it is spilling ever farther down the canyon, with unplanned building eating up every available slope. Sadly, when we visited, the white-capped Mount Illimani, which normally makes for a thrilling, photogenic backdrop, was obscured by rain clouds.

But the combined population of La Paz and neighboring El Alto is over 2.3 million, and together they are crammed into a place without level ground, and no money or ability to create effective public transport. When we arrived in El Alto, the main road to La Paz was dug up for over five kilometers, so we just resorted to riding our big knobby-tired BMWs along the roadworks, ignoring the puzzled onlookers scurrying out of the way.

It seems that the citizens of El Alto are fed up with the road projects, too. When I tried to take a cab

Colorful and crowded, Bolivia's capital city sits nearly 12,000 feet above sea level, about two hundred feet shy of the highest capital city, Lhasa, Tibet.

Making lemonade from lemons: One British company's delivery mistake influenced the entire history of Bolivian women's fashion. Hats off to this *cholita*'s statement!

to a famous overlook, every road out was blocked with demonstrations by local organizers campaigning against the mayor. "Less money on roads and more money on education," was the basic message. Luckily, I got out of there before rush hour.

That is not to say that the city isn't trying to do something about mass transit. If you cannot dig a metro or lay railway lines or build freeways, where can you go? You go UP. The city now has three working lines of the Mi Teleférico cable car system that looks like it ought to be running up a swanky Swiss ski slope; it's the longest and highest urban cable car system in the world. The pylons take up almost no room, the system is quiet and nonpolluting, and the sensation of flying above the chaos is electrifying. I rode it up to the edge of El Alto, then all the way back to the south side of the city. Very impressive.

What we enjoyed about the Perúvian mountain roads, Bolivia does even better. Twisty, dangerous, and scenic . . . and in the Cordillera Quimsa Cruz they're dirt as well.

DAY 35
NATURAL BEAUTY VS. UGLY REALITY

This is the story of how I got assaulted by a drunk woman in Cohoni, Bolivia.

Of the six countries we were visiting on this journey, Bolivia is by far the poorest. For comparison, the GDP per capita of the United States is $57,000. Chile and Argentina are both about half that of the United States, while Perú, Colombia, and Ecuador are half of Chile and Argentina. Bolivia is half again, at $6,000. It's pretty safe to assume that most of the people we met while we were riding through the Cordillera Quimsa Cruz, south of La Paz, were living lives economically well below that of their average countrymen. Many are likely living on subsistence farming, where they're not even counted in the GDP because no economic activity is generated.

South of La Paz, we rode along the Río Choqueyapu through a valley of small farms, and then climbed up a number of spectacular mountain passes where people were scratching out a living on ever-smaller and -higher terraces. These beautiful mountains and valleys filled the horizon for hundreds of miles, and we gaped at them as we tracked around the snow-capped Nevada Illimani.

The road was made of dirt but well maintained, and we shortly came across a large road crew grading and repairing the surface. When they spotted our group of gringos on large bikes, they decided it was too good an opportunity to pass up and blocked our path. They were demanding a toll—literally, highway robbery. After a lot of back and forth, we settled on 50

A potentially dangerous situation can also yield the most epic travel story if you keep your wits about you. These fine men stopped us for a bribe, so we paid them—and lived to tell the tale a thousand times.

bolivianos as payment (about $8 US) to the old gentleman leading the negotiation. There were at least 20 others in this group, so we have no idea how the bounty was eventually divided up. We heard later that the cash likely went into a community fund, but I'm not so convinced.

In Cohoni we stopped for snacks at the only café in town. As usual, a group of school kids swarmed around to ask what we were doing, and we handed out business cards with a map of the ride. At the other end of the plaza was a group of men and women sitting in the shade of the church, passing around a large bottle of local moonshine. They had obviously been at it for a while, and were all very drunk. I went over to chat, but declined a glass of the booze they offered me. One of the ladies, who was very well turned-out, in traditional clothes and a bowler hat, asked me to take a picture with her. She was well the worse for the alcohol, but still confided to me that I should not talk to the men, *"pero son todos borrachos,"* or, because they are all drunkards. So far it was all good fun,

but then she said I should pay her for the photo, as it was going "all around the world." That last part was correct.

I gave her a couple of coins, but she thrust them back at me, saying she wanted 50 bolivianos. Then the guy with the bottle chimed in, saying they wanted 100 bolivianos. When I politely refused, a bunch of them grabbed my camera. Mind you, these are people who were used to manual labor, and they had very firm grips. I made it very clear that they were getting neither 100 bolivianos nor my camera, but arguing with drunks is usually a one-sided conversation. With help from my friends, I eventually secured the camera and started to walk away, but not before the old lady ran after me and pounded angrily on my back—presumably because she was too short to reach my head.

The darker footnote to this was that one of the little girls ran over and, with an air of resignation, grabbed the arm of the man with the bottle to lead him away from the fracas. She was being asked to be adult long before she should have been.

BOLIVIA

DAY 35
SIN HISTORIA, NO FUTURA

While the rest of the team pores over their GPS routes, host Hans Hesse casually unfolds an analog map and points out the most scenic way to Uyuni.

On our first night out of La Paz, we stayed in the guest house and bunkhouse on Tenería Ranch that's been in Hans Hesse's family for generations. He and his family welcomed us with open arms and made a fantastic dinner of roast pork, local vegetables, and fresh bread, all prepared in their huge outdoor oven.

We chatted for a while, which was as much a test of his patience as my Spanish; he wearing an Oakland A's baseball hat, for which there was no explanation. Hans was born on this farm 80-odd years ago and, until the age of seven, only spoke Aymara, learned from his grandmother. He moved to La Paz for college, and then moved to Germany to work for a manufacturer of heavy-lifting machinery on the docks at Kiel and Bremen. He had traveled often to the United States on business. He must have done all right, as he retired at age 46 and, because "the pension was not paid until age 65," moved back to the family farm, where it was cheaper to live.

He told me about his four kids, the Chinese motorbike that he still rides, and the buildings on the farm that dated back 600 years. He bemoaned the fact that the original buildings, whose foundations could still be seen through the grass, were perfectly aligned to catch the winter and summer sun on different walls, but were torn down anyway.

Don Hans then described the family memorial on the property, which predates the arrival of the Spanish and was originally written in Aymara, converted to Quechua, then finally Catholicized to include a cross and a niche for a statue of the Virgin. Don Hans told me that the bones of many ancestors on his mother's side are interred here, as he expects his to be in time.

He is very proud of the clean air and good living in the mountains; he offered that the air is so clear that in the '90s they used to regularly see UFOs. He explained, "It must have been true, as they said so on the radio."

I thanked him for taking the time to share his stories and family history. He thanked me for taking an interest, and ended with, "*Sin historia, no futura*."

Without a history, you don't have a future.

BOLIVIA

Scenes from Tenería Ranch, a secret gem our local guide Sergio revealed. Remote, rustic, and cosmopolitan, an entire (other) book can be written about this place.

With no official markings across the Salar, the "dark roads" are your only means of knowing which way it is to the nearest "shore" town.

DAY 38
LIKE SAILING WITHOUT CURRENTS

The Salar de Uyuni is 4,000 square miles of evaporated salt, plopped in the Altiplano of southern Bolivia. The world's largest salt flat is perfectly flat to within one meter over its entire extent, though we did have a discussion on geodesics and gravity after I got the question, "If it is entirely flat, how come you can see the curvature of the Earth?"

The solid surface is rock hard and forms distinctive hexagonal tiles with raised edges that are a function of the crystalline structure of the salt. That surface is remarkably hard and sharp; if you fell off your bike at speed, it would be like landing on the world's biggest and sharpest belt sander. You would be shredded. And goodness knows how much we shortened the lives of our bike tires.

We had the opportunity to spend the night camping on Isla del Pescado, surrounded by salt and a beautiful sunset. To get there we rode across the untracked salt from the north side of the ancient lake at Jirira, and then east to get to "dry land" again at Colchani; crossing the area from northwest to southeast added up to a 125-mile voyage. For both legs, the best way to navigate is by compass, and by holding a constant heading. It's just like sailing, except you do not have to allow for currents or tides.

The serious dare here is to peg the throttle in top gear and keep your eyes closed for five minutes, but I decided this would have to stay on my bucket list a little while longer. The easier challenge is to write your name on the salt and record it on your GPS tracker.

Regardless of which dare you took, by the end of the day all the bikes were caked in a substantial layer of salt that had to be thoroughly washed off. Once our group showed up, the car washes in Uyuni began to really start humming.

100

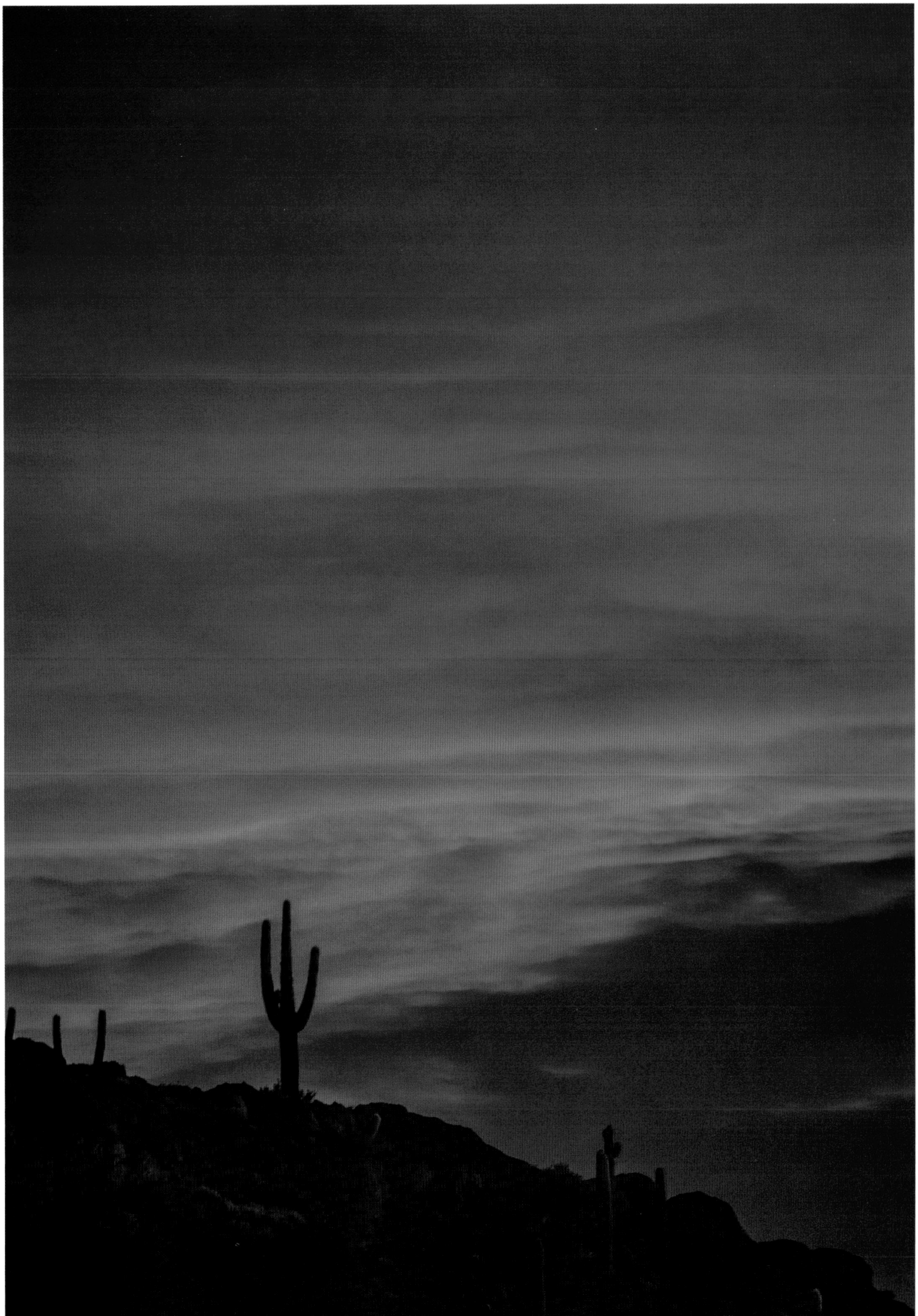

From his penthouse tent perch on Isla del Pescado, photographer Alfonse Palaima can literally see for miles and miles across the Salar.

With more than 4,000 square miles of dry lake to ride at nearly 12,000 feet above sea level, getting both lost and dizzy are normal on the Salar de Uyuni.

DAY 39

RIDING THE RUSTED RAILS

The railways in the countries we have visited so far are there to service minerals, not people.

Building railways in the Andes is not a very practical proposition in the first place, as exports are more important than public transport, and the major population centers are set in some very challenging geography: La Paz and Quito, for instance, are located in deep valleys, which is terrific for sheltering them from the wind, but makes it almost impossible to lay down tracks.

Bolivia's railway network started out with a plan to connect the mines through Uyuni, in the Altiplano, to the coastal port of Antofagasta. At the time, that city was part of Bolivia but, after the War Of the Pacific in the 1880s, involving Perú, Bolivia, and Chile (over the railways), Bolivia ceded Antofagasta to Chile and became a land-locked nation.

The rails were built, equipped, and operated by British companies floated on the London Stock Exchange. Uyuni is still a rail crossroads, but a collapse of the

Just a few kilometers from the center of Uyuni is a railway graveyard featuring the huge rusted remnants of British mining efforts from over a century ago.

mining industry in the 1940s resulted in dozens of steam engines and railcars being simply abandoned on a spur outside the city. Some of these engines are a hundred years old, and are being gradually etched away by the salt air, or pillaged to sell for scrap.

We had time to make a quick lunch stop here, so photographer Alfonse and I found some shade inside the firebox of one old locomotive. As we were leaving, we saw that one of the tour operators was clearly upset that we had ridden our off-road-capable machines right up to the line of rusting hulks. Hey, man, we thought—this is a scrapyard, not the Smithsonian.

One small footnote: The ladies in Bolivia wearing traditional dress, called *cholitas*, all wear dandy little bowler hats, and how they wear them sends a signal about marital status. If it's level, the wearer is married; at a jaunty angle means single or widowed. These hats arrived in Bolivia and were originally meant for railway engineers, but, when too many small sizes came in the shipment, an enterprising salesman peddled them to the local ladies, who thought they were cool and practical. It obviously caught on, judging by what we've seen here a century later.

BOLIVIA

With every border crossing comes a litany of office visits, and paperwork, and in Bolivia, it's no different. It's just more scenic. Really.

DAY 41
HALFWAY THERE–LEAVING BOLIVIA
Leaving Bolivia

Expedition 65 set out to cross 65 degrees of latitude in 65 days. We left Cartagena, Colombia, at 10 degrees N on September 7, and we are now in San Pedro de Atacama, Chile, at 23 degrees S. Half of our 65 degrees are now completed.

We have visited four countries Colombia, Ecuador, Perú, and Bolivia and each one has been a challenge in its own way, but Bolivia definitely presented the hardest and most challenging riding. We have ridden many, many roads that have been substantially more dangerous than the Death Road near La Paz, but we are still here regrouping in San Pedro.

In Bolivia we had some very special moments with some amazing people. A small sample:

- To get from the customs entry point near Copacabana, Bolivia, to the capital, La Paz, you have to cross a narrow part of Lake Titicaca on a fleet of independently operated barges that carry every size of vehicle. Riding a big bike onto a lurching barge, and then getting off backwards has been one of the most unique challenges so far.

- Tiberio and I took shelter in the shade of a house and chatted to the owner, Juan Paco. He told us about his farming operation, how he got tomatoes and peaches to market in La Paz, and then, without pause, he told us about his plans for an expansion into grapes, and would we American investors like

108

The riding near Polques Hot Springs had us going into and out of the sulfuric mist—but just for our own amusement.

to work with him to provide external financing. Juan Paco—future Bolivian Entrepreneur of the Year.

- Donna Lupe and her family run a hostel on the edge of the Salar de Uyuni, and somehow managed to house 16 people when we just showed up out of the blue at 9:30 at night. It was a crappy pile of dusty bricks from the outside, but a comfortable, warm, and clean space on the inside. Never judge a hostel by its exterior.

- We exited Bolivian Customs at the world's highest customs post, which sits at 16,508 feet. The crew there could not have been more pleasant and helpful, but I have no idea why there is a customs post at the end of a 10 km one-way road next to a borax mine.

- At Polques Hot Springs, where we stayed at a refuge overnight, we met a German couple and their five-year-old boy who had cycled down from Cartagena. They were eight months on the road and still heading south, up and down the Andes. Amazing.

As we were leaving Polques, the six-year-old daughter of the family that ran the place started to do the laundry. Her father fetched a barrel of hot water from the spring, and she just got to work scrubbing and cleaning.

This has truly been an amazing glimpse into other people's lives.

BOLIVIA

CENTRAL **6** ANDES

PROVINCIA DE SALTA

Regrouping in San Pedro
de Atacama, the entire
team crosses together
into Argentina.

DAY 43
LA HOSPITALIDAD ARGENTINA

When our group assembled in Cartagena to begin this trip, we met Jorge Jovanovics for the first time. We had intended to camp along most of the route, and Jorge was joining us as the team cook. The truth of the matter is we ended up camping much less than planned, but Jorge worked miracles in all the places we spent our nights anyway—commandeering the kitchens of hostels, setting up a working food prep area on freezing Altiplano sites—to produce astonishing, wholesome meals in the most challenging conditions.

More than that, Jorge threw himself into helping the effort in any way, and became a true collaborator in the planning of Expedition 65. We could not have functioned without Jorge.

Last night, we passed by Jorge's hometown and were invited to dinner by his family in Campo

Quijano, near Salta, Argentina. Little did we know what was in store. Jorge's father, Jorge Sr., presided over a huge barbecue, and his mother, Leonor, prepared dessert for the Expedition 65 team and their large extended family.

After a 300-mile day across the cold, desolate Andes, followed by a Ruta 40 slog that required us to navigate 15 miles of construction in the dark, we fell on all this food and wine like a pack of starved wolves. Afterward, it wasn't much of a stretch to slip from food coma to deep sleep, so we were fortunate that the family graciously allowed us to crash at their property.

Jorge, thanks so much for opening your house to this dusty, dirty group of gringos. We will remember this evening for a long time.

114

Your typical Argentinian meat festival: Tenderloin, skirt steak, blood sausage and more.

Near Salta, Argentina, three generations of Jovanovics opened up their home to us for their weekly family dinner.

Running parallel to the Pacific coastline of South America for nearly its entire length is a wall of mountains known as the Andes. We zigzagged across these peaks for more than 4,000 miles en route to the end of the world.

MOUNTAINS ARE BIG—THEY DON'T FIT INTO A CAMERA

The highest peak in North America is Denali (Mount McKinley) in Alaska, at 20,310 feet. But the Andes can boast 46 mountains taller than Denali, and as we wound our way south, we'd been privy to a peak-fest that simply would not stop.

In Perú we stayed at Huaraz, right under Huascarán (22,204 feet), while in Ecuador we rode around Chimborazo (20,565 feet) and experienced the extreme climate-altering power of these mountains for ourselves; a dry, arid environment on the downwind side, but humid and full of greenery on the other.

In Bolivia the view of La Paz was dominated by Illimani, a mountain that provides a glorious, 21,204-foot backdrop.

Crossing from Chile into Argentina across the high,

arid Puna de Atacama, we passed Llullaillaco (don't even try to pronounce this one), where archaeologists recently discovered Incan sacrificial sites on the summit.

In Barreal, Argentina, we stayed in a ranch house on the Río de los Patos river with a view from the backyard that included Aconcagua (the highest peak in the Americas at 22,841 feet) and Mercedario (20,570 feet). Not a bad scene to wake up to, eh?

The trouble with all these prime peaks, however, is the impossibility of doing them justice—photographically, anyway. As we rode down into Barreal and the peaks came into view after we cleared the canyon, the impression was truly breathtaking—but mostly disappointing when seen in a photo.

You just had to be there.

Our filmmaker, Sterling Noren, was normally saddled with the complex duty of documenting our journey via video, so this brief moment where he found himself shooting with "only" two cameras felt like true freedom.

DARWIN WAS HERE

These bottles are left along the roadside
all over Argentina as shrines to the
victims of auto accidents.

As we crossed the pre-Cordillera into Mendoza, Argentina, and got an in-your-face view of the towering Andes—which have to be scaled to get to Chile—we could not help but have a new appreciation for the tenacity of the earliest travelers to these parts.

One of those was Charles Darwin. In 1831, the 22-year-old recent graduate embarked on the HMS *Beagle* as a naturalist for a surveying voyage from the UK. The trip was planned for two years, but would last five, and Darwin paid his own way (with help from his father's brother-in-law Josiah Wedgwood, of fine pottery fame) so that he could maintain control over anything he collected. He saw his role more as companion to Captain Robert FitzRoy, rather than scientific explorer, but both these ideas changed quickly as he learned more about FitzRoy, as well as the natural world he would be documenting.

By 1835, relations between the erratic FitzRoy and Darwin had reached a low point, and the men decided they needed some alone time. While the *Beagle* was anchored at Valparaíso, Chile, Darwin decided to take a month-long trip to Mendoza with 10 mules, one horse, and two guides. In the previous month he had seen the eruption of Mount Osorno, and had been on the ground at Valdivia when one of the worst earthquakes to hit Chile leveled the town.

At that time, scientists saw themselves more as broad thinkers and investigators. Darwin had observed that some nearby mussel beds had risen a couple of feet after the earthquake, which led him to agree with Charles Lyell's theory that the earth was not formed by huge upheavals (vulcanology), but by little changes over a huge length of time. As Andy Dufresne says in *The Shawshank Redemption*, "Geology: just pressure and time."

Current-day Mendoza is a delightful place that's the center of Argentina's wine industry, but back then, Darwin called it "a forlorn and stupid town." On his travels here, he passed the same road we used. Along the way, there is an almost invisible memorial to the fact that Darwin discovered fossilized sequoia trees that could not have grown at this 9,000 foot elevation, but must have been, like the mussels, pushed here by massive forces over an unimaginable period of time.

He did not publish any of this until years later, but on the bicentennial of his birth (1809) and the

This remote plaque off a dirt road commemorates the 200th anniversary of Charles Darwin's birth in 2009, and also marks the 150th anniversary of his famous tome, *The Origin of Species*.

150th anniversary of the publication of *The Origin of Species* (1859), a plaque was erected at the supposed spot of this discovery. The original plaque was vandalized by creationists, so a larger, thicker version replaced it, but this still has to be the most remote and unheralded monument I have ever visited. It's stuck in the middle of 60 miles of dirt road next to a worked-out silver mine.

In a 2002 poll commissioned by the BBC for the program, *100 Greatest Britons*, Charles Darwin was ranked fourth behind Churchill, Brunel, and Lady Di—so maybe the list was a product of the time. He was honored by being put to rest in Westminster Cathedral in 1882, but a memorial in the remoteness of the Argentine Andes also seems very fitting.

The last few miles between Uspallata and Mendoza are spectacular in every way, making it very difficult to keep your eyes on the road.

Refreshed from a day of rest in the Mendoza wine region, some of us got a little too excited to be back on the road—and we picked up a few minor infractions.

DAY 49
THE FIRST TRAFFIC TICKET

We have now collectively ridden over 100,000 miles on the Expedition 65 trek, and every one of us has committed every imaginable traffic violation hundreds of times. We have broken speed limits, ridden the wrong way on one-way streets, and it is impossible to calculate how many times we have overtaken other vehicles across double yellow lines. Bad roads, big hills, slow, diesel-spewing trucks, erratic buses—you just have to get past them all, and very quickly. If we had followed the law, we probably wouldn't even be out of Colombia yet.

So it really is amazing that it was seven weeks before we got a ticket.

Leaving Mendoza to cross the Andes to Santiago, Chile, there is a nice highway with great visibility, lots of trucks, and a perfect spot for the local police to park and wait for drivers to cross the double yellow

lines. Sterling Noren and I were at the back of the pack when we decided to sweep past a bus—and right into the arms of the law.

We tried the "We don't speak any Spanish" routine (they spoke English), and we tried the "Surely we can pay the fine now, Officer" (they were not shaking us down and did not want a bribe), but eventually they took our driver's licenses, gave us tickets for offenses described as *gravisíma* ("extremely serious"), and told us to go to the nearest bank to pay—and only then would we get our licenses back. The nearest bank was a 25-mile ride to Uspallata, where we paid the $300 fine and rode back to collect our documents.

Considering the cost of the fine divided by the total number of undetected offenses we had committed on this road trip so far, it really wasn't such a bad deal.

Some of us were able to explore the city of Santiago, but the camera crew drew the short straw and spent nearly 12 hours watching two men service a dozen motorcycles.

With more than 7,000 miles clocked, our motorcycles were in sore need of a rest day. Installing the new rubber and fluids was left to the professionals at MotoAventura.

DAY 50
TWO MISSIONS FOR THE DAY

Santiago, Chile—Today's To-Do List:
Get an oil change.
Get a haircut.
Check. And check.

At MotoAventura, Thomas and Mauro did a fantastic job changing our oil, swapping in new tires, and replacing our oil and air filters, all in an hour. Both are motorbike fanatics—Mauro is from Santiago and showed up on the most immaculate Honda sportbike I've seen, and Thomas is a German who moved here

years ago with his Chilean wife. In the background of the shop is a poster of the Motorex oil we are all using for this trip.

As for the hair, well, I had wandered into a downmarket shopping center near our hotel and found Omar in a small salon on the lower level, where he's worked for 30 years. Once we started chatting, it came out that one of his clients is the publisher of *Off Road*, a magazine I take great interest in back home.

Small world.

DAY 51
A RARITY IN SOUTH AMERICA

The usual geographic profile of the cities that we have crossed so far is that of a wealth pyramid. In the center there is money, history, sanity, and (relative) safety, but as you head outward, the population's economic status falls exponentially, until, at the edges, you see the primitive, broken, and desperate; the struggling people, the choking diesels, and the burning garbage.

Quito and La Paz follow this model, but the worst was Lima, the capital of Perú, where there's a square mile or two of "normality" surrounded by 50 miles of unplanned development, chaotic transport, and miserable conditions in every direction. These cities have virtually no public transportation and appear to have nothing remotely resembling a building code or city plan.

I assumed this was the model for all of South America—until we rolled into Santiago, Chile. Here is a beautiful, thoroughly livable city, jammed up against a lovely backdrop of the snow-covered Andes. We did not ride into a perimeter of slums to get into the inner city, but through well-built suburbs, with decent shopping on main roads that were pothole-free and safe at high speeds. The avenues are wide and pleasant, and there are dozens of open-air cafés with every imaginable food choice.

The city also feels youthful and vibrant. Maybe that's no accident, as Santiago's nickname is "Chile-con Valley," after a program that has created a Silicon Valley-type entrepreneurial culture. The United States seems to turn away new talent while Chile is welcoming them with incentives and investment to try and diversify its economy. The majority of the companies nurtured by Start-Up Chile in Santiago have origins in the United States, with homegrown companies coming in second.

One reason the city is so functional and pleasant is probably due to its metro system; the network handles 2.4 million rides a day. I couldn't resist taking a trip, and it felt like being on a train in Paris or London—the system even won a mention as the "Best Underground in the Americas" recently. The traffic in Santiago at rush hour is still horrendous, but imagine what the city would look like if another couple of million people were on the streets trying to get around in cars.

Actually, I know exactly what it would look like—Lima.

It seems like every great nation with a highway system and lots of ground to cover has a Route Number 5—and Chile is no exception.

DAY 52

RUTA 5, CHILE: MEET *I-5*, OREGON

When you travel to a new place, your mind naturally tries to relate to a familiar experience. You think, "this mountain is like the Rockies, this road is like riding in Eastern Oregon, and oh look, they have McDonalds, too."

But in the last seven weeks of crisscrossing the Andes over six countries, I have never had a déjà vu moment; the scale, the colors, the smells, the people, the roads, and the customs I've encountered have all been completely disorienting, fascinating, and overwhelming. Until now.

Leaving Santiago, Chile, we jumped on the freeway to expedite our journey south, so we could cover six degrees of latitude in one day. Ruta 5 was exactly the same experience for me as riding on I-5 through Oregon. The road leads down through a wide fertile valley with orchards, wineries, and pine forests, with the familiar smells of agriculture and logging. We passed 18-wheelers hauling logs and wood chips,

and saw signs for wine tours. The roadside billboards were for fertilizer and farm machinery. The vegetation changed from high desert to corn and grapes and yellow mustard seed and sod farms and evergreens surrounded by yellow Scotch broom. The valley is edged on the east side by a row of high, snow-capped volcanoes formed by the subduction of the Pacific plate colliding with South America, and on the west side, a lower Coast Range to protect the valley from the Pacific.

Welcome home.

One thing that was not the same were the fees. Ruta 5 is a toll road that more closely resembles a French autoroute, with regular infuriating toll booths, but also an immaculate, well-maintained road surface and frequent, excellent gas stations with great service and food. Interstate 5 in the United States would not earn any awards for service, surface, or safety. America—please learn from Chile.

Some of our group were on the fast track, so they missed these gorgeous waterfalls in the countryside and got to tailgate logging trucks instead.

Not every day turned out as planned. A weather-impacted rest day in Trevelin had us saying goodbye to two of our best travel mates. Here, Chris White wishes us the best for our journey to the end of the world.

DAY 55
TWO LESS TO THE FINISH LINE

Bill Whitacre and Chris White will have to leave today. Our accumulated delays mean they have to break off before our trip's conclusion to get home on time. I will miss both of these gentlemen.

When you travel with a group of guys for seven weeks, you inevitably reveal something of yourself that is not obvious to everyone else. You cannot hide your demons, and you cannot help but show your strengths. We have ridden, eaten, slept, and laughed together, and experienced highs and lows that would have wrecked a weaker group.

Bill Whitacre turned out to be a consummate leader who always sought to find the common ground whenever we had disagreements. His deadpan sense of humor could disarm the most contentious situation and break the ice with any stranger. He had handled all the money on this trek, and now that he's

gone, we will probably spend what's left like drunken sailors. Bill professes to be a careful guy, but was ready to do ANYTHING if it would increase the epic factor on an already epic trip. Bill always thinks the potatoes are "really, really good." Bill is also not a good mechanic.

Chris White is the youngest member of the group, but always showed the most mature and interesting ways to think about any new issue. He has been ready to pitch in with anything, and I am particularly grateful for his time riding sweep and helping me get out of a very threatening day in the deep sand in Bolivia. He spent almost a week riding on a totally destroyed rear shock, with not a single word of complaint. Chris is frank and smart and charming. Chris will make a great father to his soon-to-be-born child.

Safe travels, Bill and Chris. See you soon.

Bill Whitacre also had to depart the group, which means our team will now be sorely lacking in financial management skills.

Usually the sign of a recent rainfall, this rainbow also marked the direction of our ride ahead (though once again, we broke up into teams).

Sculptor Marcelo Lopez carved burnt lenga trees into these works of art to bring attention to the natural surroundings.

DAY 56
THE CARVED WOOD

El Bosque Tallado ("The Carved Forest") is a collection of 50 works of art carved into lenga trees charred by fire high above El Bolsón, Argentina. It was the brain-child of the sculptor, Marcelo López, who wanted to bring attention to his natural surroundings and create an environment for collaboration with other local artists. The works carved into the dead trees where they stand are stunning.

The location is also perfect for an adventure bike detour; the 7.5 miles of steep dirt to get there is a real riding workout, and then you have the REAL workout, which is another three-quarters of a mile walk up a steep, jagged path to a climbers' refuge, with a spectacular view from Cerro Piltriquitrón to the town and the Cordon Nevada across the valley.

It's a great way to see the countryside along with some fine artwork, all while working off some Argentinian barbecue along the way.

The Carved Forest sculptures sit in a forest high above the town of El Bolson. The steep detour is worth the ride, especially on an adventure bike.

The wind howls so intensely in Patagonia it's often difficult to stay upright for any long stretch of time. Your momentum is tested regularly.

DAY 59
FORGET WHAT THEY SAY ABOUT WIND IN PATAGONIA

It's much worse. The winds in Patagonia are legendary. There is simply not enough landmass in this narrow point of South America to slow these howling blasts of air, called the "Roaring Forties," because of the latitude. The winds are stronger than the same gusts might be in the northern hemisphere because down here they have been blowing over water without interruption for such long distances. This is the most southerly bit of land that dares poke out into these gales.

Around here there's normally a constant 25 mph wind, which is difficult enough to ride in, but when we started our trek along this part of Ruta 40, the local weather service reported sustained 75 mph winds—which was completely insane. When there was a road surface like tarmac or solid rock to offer some grip, it was feasible to lean the bike into the gusts for a measure of stability, but with fresh gravel, it became totally impossible to resist the sideways forces—you could not lean far

No crash bar system is impervious. One small, well-placed rock can poke through a Boxer's head cover at the very worst time. Plan for that.

enough without losing all grip. Every one of us went down or got knocked off the road at some point. If you parked your bike with the side stand upwind, it would be pushed over by the wind instantly.

Everyone tried their own technique for dealing with this—either let the bike drift and then lurch upwind periodically, or lean way into the wind to keep the bike vertical, or go fast enough for the wheels to give you more gyroscopic help—but the physics won every time. We were on big bikes, and there was simply no way to curl up small enough to resist the blast force.

At one point our little group reached the end of a tiny section of pavement covered with nothing but loose gravel all the way to the horizon, with the wind blowing directly across the road. We could not even stand, let alone ride. Long story short, we left the bikes to the wind and hunkered down behind a small berm with day-old sandwiches to see if the gusts would die down. Four hours later, the wind lessened by a fraction, and we took off for another attempt. The last push managed to get us onto tarmac and finally on to El Calafate.

In all, we endured about 70 miles of this nonsense. It became a massive shared experience that strengthened the group, and a life lesson for us all. No road would seem difficult after this.

Patagonia's winds (called "The Roaring 40s" due to the latitude) are so relentless, you just learn to lean alot.

This group of Welshmen journeyed to Argentina over 200 years ago, seeking refuge from the English government. Their ancestors carry on old Welsh traditions to this day.

DAY 55
THE *MIMOSA*, OR, THE WELSH *MAYFLOWER*

Somewhere down the line my Evans ancestry goes back to Wales, so maybe I am related to the Welsh community here in Argentina. Wait, what?

The Welsh in Argentina? How did that happen?!

In the early 1800s, as the coal, slate, iron, and steel from Wales were beginning to fuel much of the Industrial Revolution, many Welshmen also started to fear that the Welsh language and culture would be in danger of being absorbed by England. Looking for places to start colonies and continue their traditions, some turned to other parts of the world. They even tried parts of the United States, but the forces of absorption there were too strong.

In 1861, a group of Welshmen struck a deal with the Argentine government for a tract of land in Patagonia. Some 200 souls departed Liverpool for Argentina aboard the sea clipper *Mimosa*. This Welsh version of the *Mayflower* was helping its passengers escape the English influence on their language, faith, and culture, much like the Pilgrims before them. An old photo of passengers on the voyage shows a dour and determined group, well past their youth; you can bet there were not a lot of laughs on this journey.

They originally settled on the coast and learned to tame the unforgiving pampas with irrigation, and the community eventually spread west to the Andes. Here in Trevelin, John Evans built a town based on wheat and flour milling, until Argentine dictator Juan Perón decided the area was not appropriate for wheat and shifted from farming to cattle ranching. I suppose dictators can do that.

In 1902 the influence of the Welsh was significant enough that, along with the indigenous Mapuche, they managed to insist on a change to the Chile–Argentina border to prevent their community from being split between two countries.

Today there are perhaps 50,000 Welsh speakers here in Chubut Province. They even hold four annual Eisteddfod festivals—Gaelic gatherings for dance, music, and poetry in the Welsh language. It is hard for me to reconcile that photo of the serious *Mimosa* passengers with a group of people whose motivation to escape the English was to dress as druids to sing, dance, and recite poetry.

The author is pretty sure that this street sign in
Chubut Province, Argentina, is a tribute to a long-
lost relative from Wales.

The ride along the Carretera Austral is spectacular, but as we zigzagged between Chile and Argentina so many times, we often lost track of which country we were in.

DAY 57
THE CARRETERA AUSTRAL

Southern Chile is so huge and beautiful and rugged and difficult, it can only sustain a small number of remote communities scattered in the steep mountains and forest and fjords.

Construction of the Carretera Austral ("Southern Highway") was started in 1976 under the dictatorship of Augusto Pinochet as an attempt to connect this complex part of the country without needing to go over to Argentina and back again. Starting at Puerto Montt and running 800 miles south, the road wasn't completed until the section to Villa O'Higgins opened

in 2000, and even now, it only connects about 100,000 people. This whole area is practically uninhabited.

We got a chance to ride a small part of the road as we dropped into Puyuhuapi and then down to Cerro Castillo, close to Lake General Carrera. The ride through the mountains and glacial valleys and along the fjords is truly spectacular, with the road switching from impeccable sweeping tarmac to crushed rock with potholes. Dust was not a problem in this wet and cold season, but the rain clouds robbed us of some of the most spectacular views.

With the impending warm weather slowly pushing winter higher into the hills, the mountains give up their snowmelt. Springtime in Patagonia is a raw and beautiful sight.

DAY 60
METEOROLOGY AND BUREAUCRACY

The Andes control everything in South America—trade, travel, national identity, industry, history, religion, and most importantly, climate.

In the northern half of the continent, the winds blow from the east and pick up megatons of warm Atlantic water, that is in turn blocked by the Andes. This creates Amazonia on one side of the range and the Atacama Desert on the other: the world's wettest and driest places right next to each other. In the southern half, the winds blow from the west, over the cold Pacific and even colder Humboldt Current. They then pick up cold water that the Andes have been trapping for eons to make the glaciers, fjords, and forests in southern Chile. There's nothing left for Argentina then, but the Patagonian wind.

When we crossed from Chile to Argentina, west to east, the wind was howling. Lake General Carrera spans the border, with the permanent snow, rain, and rainbows rolling over the mountains in the west and leaving cloudless skies and gales in the east. The

plants we saw in Chile were pines, ferns, and the grasses cattle grazed on. In Argentina, any plant that ever stuck its head up more than a few inches had been clipped by the wind and the process of natural selection in this hostile ecosystem. In similar fashion, the animal kingdom here is represented by hardy hares, guanacos, and armadillos.

But then there is the bureaucracy.

Most of the time, border crossings between Chile and Argentina are well organized and co-located, with both nations working together to make the crossing as easy as possible for their citizens. Sometimes, however, the posts can be miles apart. On one crossing we managed to miss the Chile Carabinieri post in town and had to ride 15 miles on a treacherous road in 55-mile-per-hour winds—only to be told to go back and get our passports stamped on the other side. As both posts were still making duplicates using carbon paper, this was not a rapid process.

But then, we did get to admire the spectacular view three times. Life has its compensations.

NALCA, THE JURASSIC RHUBARB

The prehistoric (and utterly unique) nalca plant thrives in southern Chile, where it's a common snack among the locals (but not the author).

Riding the Carretera Austral in southern Chile seems strangely familiar to those of us who live at the same latitude north of the Equator. The temperatures and constant rain and colors and smells and plants are what we would expect to see at 45 degrees near the Pacific; all those pines, yellow Scotch broom, ferns, and flowering lupines.

But one plant stands out as completely distinctive. *Nalca*, known as Chilean rhubarb (though it is not related to rhubarb), is unique to the area and seems to thrive in these environs. This prehistoric plant evolved 150 million years ago in the late Jurassic period—so it would have been familiar to dinosaurs and to Fred Flintstone—and has adapted to the poor soil, growing larger than most of its competition. Because it is crammed with nutritional goodness, the young shoots are eaten in these parts quite regularly, often after being peeled and dipped in salt, or made into jams.

DAY 61
TORRES DEL PAINE–GEOLOGY AND HOSPITALITY

We had no place to stay that first snowy night in Chile, but the kind folks at Hotel Tres Pasos unlocked its doors, pointed the way to the bar, and served us an epic meal.

We crossed into Chile with high expectations, and no reservations, in Torres del Paine National Park. The hostels were either closed or full, the famous hotels and lodges were crazily expensive, and the rain was rolling all over us. After a couple of phone calls, we found Hotel Tres Pasos, which wasn't supposed to open for another week, but, after sweet-talking the staff and then the owner—who drove 25 miles to talk to us—they unlocked their doors for our group, threw more logs on the fire, opened the bar, and cooked us a stupendous salmon and steak dinner. It was the warmest possible welcome for a group of cold, dripping wet, and tired riders.

The following morning, we brushed the new snow off our bikes and headed out to the park to soak up the scenery. To describe the sights as spectacular doesn't even come close. The mountains here are the result of sedimentary and granite layers being pushed up and eroded by glaciers and wind and time, leaving behind a dramatic, jagged landscape. The views of the Torres del Paine ("Towers of Blue") behind the Laguna Amarga, and the view of the Cuernos del Paine across Lake Pehoé from the Explora Lodge are especially magnificent.

The sun breaks through at last as we trace the edges of Torres del Paine National Park.

The visuals in Torres del Paine National Park are simply out of this world, with glaciers, jagged stone peaks, and turquoise-blue waters all competing for your attention. It's hard to describe the beauty.

With snowfall putting a damper on our ride plan, we take the time to catch up on emails and empty a few bottles of local Carménère.

Having lived in Perú for several years, our van driver Adam Timm felt pretty comfortable with the vibe in Patagonia, too.

When you're surrounded by natural wonders and icy roads, and only two days from the trip's endpoint, sometimes it's okay to stay put for an extra day.

165

We quickly struck up a friendship with this truck driver on the ferry when he told us he used to ride motorbikes, too.

DAY 62
BIKE BROTHERHOOD

While we were waiting at the ferry station to cross the Straits of Magellan to Tierra del Fuego, all our fellow passengers wanted to chat about the bikes and where we were going. One truck driver pointedly asked about our ages, and joked that this trip seemed like a big effort for guys of our vintage.

We introduced ourselves to Daniel , the gentleman driving the big white Scania. I asked him his age, to which he replied, "54." Then I told him that the three guys he was talking to were 6, 10, and 13 years older

than him, and still having a blast riding the length of the continent on big adventure bikes.

He then produced a couple of faded pictures from a photo album he kept in the cab, one showing him on a custom Yamaha 400 2-stroke from 36 years ago, which he claimed he could wheelie 100 yards at a time. Apparently his biking days are over, but he still had a huge glint in his eye after getting the chance to relive those years with others who truly understood his exhilaration.

DAY 62
MAGELLAN AND PATAGONIA

One of our groups got separated from the other at the Straits of Magellan ferry crossing, so we found ourselves with time to poke around the area—where we found this plaque.

Now we have completed the final leg of our journey across the Straits of Magellan from Patagonia to Tierra de Fuego, and back into Argentina. We are almost to Ushuaia.

The ferry trip across the narrow strait was very fast, friendly, and professional, though it was definitely a challenge to ride a big bike onto the ferry across the surf, and then off again in the howling crosswind that is the norm here. The bottom line is you have to commit, or get wet.

The first European to explore this area was Ferdinand Magellan, a Portuguese navigator working for the Spanish king to find a back door into Asia. He was the first to circumnavigate the globe in 1521, and found this protected passage around the cape that now bears his name.

Magellan also named Patagonia as well. There are different accounts of how Patagonia got its name, but the most plausible is the simplest; Magellan was a big fan of the popular Spanish novel by Francisco Vásquez whose title character, Patagón, was a savage giant. Shakespeare had also stolen characters from this book and reworked them for use in *The Tempest*.

When Magellan's crew first met the native Tehuelche Indians, they were struck by how much taller these people were than Europeans and, like all sailors stories about storms and monsters that get exaggerated, the Indians were subsequently described as giants, and called Patagóns.

Around this time, the Spanish Conquistadors were starting their push onto the continent from the east and the north, but not in the 300 years of Spanish rule of South America did they bother to conquer Patagonia. It makes sense when you think about it; there was no gold to mine, no civilizations to plunder, and it is damned cold and windy—so why bother? It was left to newly independent Chile and Argentina to subject the Mapuche and Tehuelche indians in the 1830s. Eventually the Mapuche overran the Tehuelche in the east, and now they are all but decimated as a people. The original Patagóns no longer exist.

PATAGONIA

With air temperatures just above freezing and heavy winds pushing the ship around, the simple act of riding up this ferry ramp proved to be more exciting than it looks.

A fascinating historical stop at the museum dedicated as a memorial to the Falklands War and its veterans.

DAY 63

GOOD WAR OR BAD WAR, HONOR THOSE WHO SERVED

My father served in a bad war. He was conscripted in 1943 and joined the Army Corps of Signals and then volunteered to join the relatively new Airborne Division. He missed the action in Europe and was sent to Palestine as part of the British Mandate, serving as a Red Beret until he was demobilized, and the State of Israel was declared in 1948. His contemporaries returned home to a hero's welcome after the defeat of Germany; he returned unheralded after a perceived defeat in Palestine and was never the same afterwards.

Many who fought for Argentina in the Falklands War must have felt a similar emotion. Today we visited the Monumento a los Héroes de Malvinas in the naval town of Río Grande in Tierra Del Fuego, Argentina. After we stopped for photographs in the cold, cutting gale, we were greeted by Jose Salas, one of 120 Malvinas veterans who maintain a vigil at the monument to honor the fallen and the veterans of this needless conflict with Britain. Each link in the chain around this monument represents one of the 648 Argentinian dead.

He then led us into the museum—self-funded by the town's veterans—that serves as a memorial to those who gave their lives. We discussed his experience and that of my dad, but Jose was very careful to explain that the monument and museum are not there to point blame at the British, but rather to remember old friends.

I could not talk to this man without a lump in my throat and a tear in my eye, thinking about my own father and his wartime experience.

In the town of Río Grande, we meet Jose Salas, one of 120 Malvinas veterans who maintain a vigil at the Falklands museum/monument.

An Argentinian and an Englishman bury the hatchet in Tierra del Fuego.

Last stop—Ushuaia. We have now clocked 10,000 miles and traveled 65 degrees of latitude.

A selfie at the End of the World should be on every rider's bucket list.

DAY 64

EXPEDITION 65—65 DEGREES OF LATITUDE IN 65 DAYS

Just as we cruised into Ushuaia, my odometer clicked over to 10,000 miles. Big sigh: we have completed traveling 65 degrees of latitude from Cartagena, Colombia, to Ushuaia, Argentina.

We have missed one of our riders, Jason Houle, who got injured back in Perú, and our compatriots who had to make their way home, Bill Whitacre and Chris White, but here we were at last. What a journey.

These challenge coins Jim Hyde made for E-65 represent the camaraderie and teamwork involved in undertaking such an arduous journey.

Exhausted but excited, our group poses for that obligatory portrait at the sign for the End of the World in Ushuaia.

NOT ALL MOMENTS GO INTO A CAMERA

With the ferries parked due to high winds, we settled in to wait it out inside the sole shop in the area. Six hours later, we finally get across the strait into Punta Arenas.

Tierra del Fuego is not quite done with us yet.

Chris and I left Ushuaia a day early to get a jump on the wind, the distance, and the ferry crossing to Punta Arenas, from where we'd be shipping our bikes home. We left in the rain, dodged a couple of storm cells and ended up at the Chile border crossing, fortunately when they were not on strike. Then it was onward across 35 miles of construction and into the wind, passing trucks and their dust the whole way. After 65 miles of arrow-straight dirt road toward Porvenir we knew there'd be a ferry, but we had no idea when it sailed.

Finally, the road lurched toward the coast and rolled around the headland. We slalomed onto 50 miles of good rocky track that plunged to the beaches then up the cliffs, past remote houses with ancient boats pulled up, in and out of bright sun, into high winds and rain, hail, and sleet. Our "Freezing Temps" lights flashed. The wind and cold would sometimes become uncomfortable, and occasionally, terrifying. At the

end of it, we found the ferry tied up and waiting for the 8:00 a.m. sailing. A hotel was quickly procured, and Chris and I were soon tucked into a couple pisco sours and lots of Carménère wine. What a blast!

The next day broke bright and very windy and, as a result, the ferry was "*suspendido indefinidamente,*" so we set off to find the other ferry that was supposedly working. We rode across the adjacent nature reserve, chasing farm animals and wild guanacos and scaring up flocks of wildfowl and sea birds. The sun was on our faces and the wind at our backs until we got to the ferry dock, only to find the sailing "suspendido indefinidamente." Of course.

Two fantastic rides and not a single photograph was taken to record either of them. They will just have to stay etched in my cerebral cortex instead of Instagram. Of course, the ferry was not going any-where, so that's one photo I took. As far as I know, it is still there.

The author finds an elusive Ruta 40 road sign. Every single South American gift shop refers to it, but you'll see few signs on the actual road.

RUTA 40—GO QUICKLY THE WORLD IS BEING PAVED

There are a few legendary roads in the world that allow you to ride the cross section of a country, and get a glimpse at real life behind the curtain away from the capital cities and tourist centers. Route 66, the Stuart Highway, the Trans-Canada, and the M1 through Hemel Hempstead. (Just threw in the last one to see if you were paying attention.)

Ruta 40 is Argentina's longest road, running almost 3,100 miles from Bolivia in the north to Río Gallegos on the Patagonian Atlantic coast. It was started as a national project in 1935 and tracks the east side of the Andes, with 27 mountain passes going across the range. As we crisscrossed the Andes in Argentina,

this was our default route. In the north, we rode it from San Antonio de los Cobres to Mendoza; in the middle from Bariloche to Trevelin; and in the south, from Perito Moreno to El Calafate, maybe 125 miles from the end of the road.

This route used to be the classic dirt-road trek, and there are still a lot of unpaved sections, but more and more is being paved. The regional governments are also sneakily relabeling roads to steer tourism to their preferred spots—la Ruta de los Siete Lagos is now labeled as Ruta 40, and the original road is called 40X, for instance. It may not be the wild road it used to be, but it's still an epic way to see the country.

Evan Firstman, our expedition's private troubadour, serenades us one last time, with the chorus: "Because of RawHyde! Because of RawHyde!"

DAY 66
PLAYTIME ISN'T OVER UNTIL THE TOYS ARE PUT AWAY

The idea that our adventure was over only sunk in when the doors closed on the two big steel shipping containers at the port of Punta Arenas, Chile.

We spent the morning collecting all our stuff and dealing with the proper documentation required to send it all home—inventorying the baggage, handing in the temporary import paperwork for the vehicles, checking the boxes, genuflecting in front of the officials. Then the two containers arrived, we uploaded

everything, and made sure it was all strapped down tightly before one more official visit, and then the lead seals were added to the doors.

This took all day, but the two dock hands that worked with us throughout the process were amazing—Pablo and Pablo worked their asses off even while taking our suggestions for making the bikes safe and secure.

I have no idea when, or if, I will see any of my stuff again.

After ten weeks on the road, everybody is ready to get off the bikes and into an airplane headed home.

But first we have to pack: Nine hours of reshuffling, documenting, scrutinizing, and securing our gear and we eventually fill two large orange shipping containers that we hope to see again some day.

8 EPILOGUE

Despite consistently extreme conditions, this trusty R 1200 GS assigned to photographer Alfonse Palaima came through like a champ.

PART OF THE ADVENTURE BUT NOT PART OF THE PLAN

Expedition 65 took a year and a half to plan, and in the process we left nothing to chance; bikes were serviced multiple times, the route and points of interest along the way were meticulously researched, logistics were double-checked, critical reservations were made, and fuel and tires were stashed at key points all the way down the continent.

So it all worked perfectly, right? WRONG. Despite everyone's best efforts, our initial battle plan didn't survive first contact with the enemy . . . er, terrain—not even close. Here are just a few of the lessons learned from the situations that did not go down quite as we envisioned.

THE THRILL OF FILM

We were all delighted to have Sterling Noren join Expedition 65 as our embedded filmmaker. Sterling is an excellent rider, a genial companion, and a very talented storyteller. But none of us (except for Sterling) even remotely understood what it would take to make a professional movie from our trip. For starters, we never really decided if we'd be compiling a glossy travelogue, or a reality show of the trials and tribulations (and injuries and breakages), or an instructional video for future adventurers to the region. In retrospect, it seems like we tried to do all of the above.

The realities of the filmmaking process can be harsh. Whenever you see a beautiful shot of adventure riders gliding through a gorgeous backdrop within an engaging story, you normally do not see the group waiting at the side of the road for the camera setup, or riding the same stretch of pavement twice because a local truck got in the shot, or arguing about how much time all this is taking, or the frustration and danger of arriving late and in the dark at the evening's destination.

Very early in the journey, we organically started to split into smaller groups and agreed that one group would be the stars (and/or extras) in the movie portion of each day's journey. I am sure that we will all be thrilled with the end result, but if you too are looking to make a film of your next adventure ride, be sure to confirm that everyone in your group is motivated and knows what to expect. We are probably lucky we are all still talking to each other.

WHERE TO SLEEP

As we were brainstorming the format for this adventure ride, it seemed logical to plan on camping more than half the time; we were all veteran campers, we would get to experience the closeness to nature, we would all save money, and there was the benefit of having the freedom to stop where we wanted. When we did camp, we experienced extraordinary moments; on an island in the Salar de Uyuni, with a staggering sunset; under the world's biggest gold mine where we were visited by the mine security staff who ended up staying for dinner; on the beach at a lake in the Chilean Andes. Once we stayed in a compound on the coast of Perú that was a cross between the clean-up day after Burning Man and a second-rate refugee camp. Memorable nights for sure, but in all two months of our trek, we ended up camping only a dozen times, and just four of those were in the wild.

There were many reasons for this, but perhaps the primary one is that there is almost no camping infrastructure in South America equivalent to that in the United States (as with our State Park system), and no camping "culture"; the local people mostly thought we were just crazy to bother. Also, hotels and hostels are plentiful, comfortable, and cheap; when a bed is $10, why hassle with the tent? And, of course, the weather was not very cooperative—tropical rain near the Caribbean, howling winds in Patagonia, and bloody freezing temperatures in the high Andes.

Then again, maybe these are all just thin excuses and most of us simply didn't want to admit that we are too damned old for all this camping shit, and not at all embarrassed to want a warm bed. Know thyself before you go.

HOW MUCH DO YOU REALLY NEED?

With the idea to camp half the time, we had all decided to bring bigger tents and serious beds that would not fit on our bikes, and to haul a trailer that was dedicated as a camp kitchen. This led to the van being seriously overstuffed with all our crap. The cascade effect came out in full display—one bad decision leads to an entire series of bad decisions and negative consequences. It became impossible to find anything in the van, bags were constantly being schlepped back and forth, the van turned out to not have room for a bike in an emergency, and all that extra, unneeded stuff served to seriously overload the van, which caused mechanical issues. The several times we had to empty the van for customs inspection or maintenance revealed the extent of our overpacking. A pickup truck and small tents packed on the bikes for emergencies might have been a better plan.

It might be a while before any of us signs on to another 65-day adventure, but we'll certainly think long and hard about these issues before launching our next trip.

BORDERS AND CUSTOMS

We ended up crossing international borders thirteen times—from the time we entered Colombia in Cartagena, to packing the bikes into containers for the journey home from Punta Arenas in Chile, 11,000 miles later. Every one of these crossings followed a familiar, four-stage formula—Customs Out, Passport Out, Passport In, Customs In—but the time required to expedite the process varied enormously. Some crossings are organized with high-speed computer systems and international cooperation with all the facilities from both countries in the same building, but some borders have their respective offices hundreds of miles apart, and use military personnel, large ledgers, and carbon-copy documents filled out by hand. Some places wanted to inspect the bikes and luggage, and a few times we had to empty the van and trailer completely and pass all our cargo through an X-ray machine, then subject it to hand inspection. Mostly though, we found officials who were helpful and just doing their jobs—there were no rip-offs or bribes or "special" taxes on the way.

We did learn a few other important lessons, too. First, don't ride with a custom plate—we had bikes bearing DAKAR and OFFRDGS plates along for our trip, and that led to a lot of confusion, especially in Chile where their computer systems expect numbers and nobody could understand why one plate read OF FROGS. Second, it was actually straightforward to follow the temporary import process for our bikes and the van—there is a process, and every customs guy knows how to do it. It works as long as you actually leave the country again. Do NOT try and sell a bike that has been imported this way. Lastly, you have to have clean originals for all your documents—the title, registration, and letter of authorization from the bank if your bike is financed. Coming into Ecuador, we discovered the van's original paperwork had been left in Cartagena. This caused enough problems that the van had to be finally "deported" under police escort. But that's a story for a longer discussion over a couple of beers.

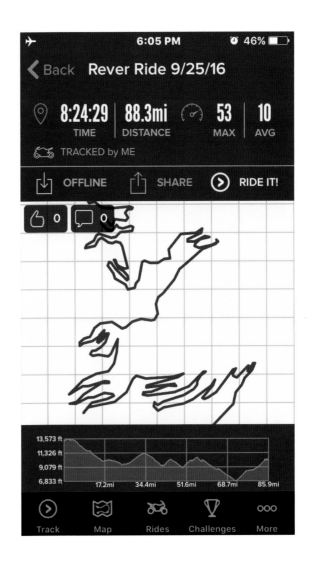

We would have been hopelessly lost on this trip were it not for our smartphones.

KNOW, THEN GO

Determining directions for each day's destination wasn't always easy. With only an end point in mind, each ride became a (mostly) enjoyable mystery. Many of the team members had Garmin GPS units mounted to their bike, but not everyone had the correct maps or routes. For those of us with global cellular packages and signals, Google helped fill in the blanks when paper maps left us guessing. Another solution that Alfonse picked up while preparing for this expedition was to download offline maps into an app called Maps.Me. Requiring minimal memory and available for download country by country, the app helped us all quickly know exactly where we were, with or without cell coverage. Map.Me also allows for GPX file import, so our "intended" routes (usually previously designed off-site) were always on display as well.

Fortunately, knowing where we'd actually ridden was much easier to glean thanks to another smartphone app called Rever. To be fair, this one also offers navigation (as well as team grouping) but requires a network to see roads and routes outside of the daily "plan." As with offline navigation on Google Maps, once you start scanning around looking for alternate routes, you'd need reconnection to a network—which is not always available in South America. In Bolivia, we spent an entire week off the grid.

Rever also picks up where the other apps leave off. You can track your ride, store the data online and share the experience with others on social media, and record it for later. Even if you never connect to a cell tower, the GPS chip in your phone will record your route distance, top speed, and time traveled. The coolest feature you get in your ride report is the elevation profile; seeing the mountain peaks and valleys in Perú alone are worth the download.

A Rever subscription will also allow for import of Butler Maps' rated and featured rides (currently only US routes).

Luis

Jorge

Sergio

HELP ALONG THE WAY

The Expedition 65 crew developed the plan for this adventure, but we were smart enough to get expert help when we had the opportunity. We would all be remiss if we did not recognize the amazing contribution of our friends in South America. And we would have been lost—literally—without them.

COLOMBIA

This beautiful country has been officially at war with the FARC rebel group since La Violencia in 1948. Though a ceasefire was signed in 2016, there are still a lot of jungle-y places that should be avoided, especially by a group of riders who are used to just jumping into the off-road wilderness without checking. We were lucky enough to get assistance from Luis Alejandro Reyes, the owner of Adventures 57. Luis provides training and tours for all corners of Colombia from his base in Bogotá, and he supplied us with recommended routes and tons of helpful advice, then set us up with his friends, so we could visit places we would have otherwise not seen. What a great way to start our ride along the continent.

ECUADOR

Jorge Cherrez and his friends in Ecuador have a motorcycle club they call the Brosters. The origin of the name is too complicated to go into here, but these guys are amazing and connected and knowledgeable and hospitable and CRAZY beyond measure. They opened up their clubhouse for the most outrageous party of the

trip and escorted us around their amazing country. The night ride in Quito, the off-road trip around Chimborazo, the food and the friendship; it's all too much to describe here. That problem about having to leave Ecuador because the van had to be deported? That too is a story for another time.

BOLIVIA

Sergio Ballivian was born in La Paz, educated in the United States and Canada, and splits his time between Bolivia and Boulder, Colorado. There are lots of streets and plazas in Bolivia named Ballivian, so I'm sure his ancestors played a role in the country's history. A former member of the National Geographic photo department, he now runs Explore Bolivia, which leads custom photo tours around the country. Sergio constructed a route that allowed us to see the wildest and toughest places in Bolivia, escorted us most of the way, and only lost his temper with the group once over our willful disobedience and incompetence on the trail—and he was right to do so.

In all three countries, we gained access to places and roads and homes and lives that would otherwise have been invisible to us. We were not tourists but guests of these gentlemen and their friends and that made the trip extra special for us all.

These folks left us with the impression that we had barely scratched the surface of their respective countries. We will all definitely return to explore the rest, and I hope we see these guys again.

MEET VICTOR SIERRA

Victor Sierra has more charm and more energy per pound than any human being I have met.

Victor is the owner of Valley Group, the company that arranged all the shipping and logistics for our bikes, our van, and our stuff, from Miami to Cartagena and back again from Punta Arenas. More than that, Victor is a keen adventure rider and joined us for the first few days of our journey through his home country of Colombia, proving to be a tireless ambassador and gracious host every step of the way.

He then flew down to join us at the end of the trip and drove with us to Ushuaia and back to the final shipping point to make sure everything was taken care of perfectly. We were held up at the ferry from Tierra del Fuego for 12 hours waiting for the wind to die down, and it was very clear that the operators were not treating motorcycles with very high priority. Somehow Victor got us and the van together on the next ferry. I have no idea how he managed to make this happen.

He's a miracle worker. We miss Victor already.

ACKNOWLEDGMENTS

Giving thanks is one of those things that doesn't cost any money, and it's worth far more than any effort to say it.

If it wasn't a dozen times a day, then it was at least hundreds of times a week that we thanked Adam Timm for—at the minimum—getting our personal belongings to each evening's final destination. Thank you. And for unloading, navigating, driving the van, supporting and simply being yourself, we thank you, Adam.

Riding shotgun in the van with Adam was Jorge Jovanovics, a miracle worker who deserves a thousand thank yous for feeding our hungry group each night. Under ever-changing conditions he rose to the challenge, even if it meant being something other than a chef—like a translator, a border crossing facilitator, or just a buddy. Thank you.

Then there's the guy who brought us all together. To the visionary and entrepreneur with the plan, and the will, to wrangle together his besties for the trip of a lifetime, we thank you, Jim Hyde! With the help of Jim's enviable skill set, we made it from the top, all the way to the bottom of an entire continent.

Fueling both the inspiration as well as the machinations involved, his idea panned out and we love him for it. Thank you!

And lastly, to the teams of people involved in producing the very book you're reading—thank you. I'll start with my old pal from the magazine publishing world, Andy Cherney, who joined the team to marry all the parts together for the build team. Thanks man. I'd also like to thank John Barnett for his creative eye designing the book and Dana Henricks for proofing the whole package. Thank you all!

Were it not for the support and persistent passion we received from Bill Whitacre and Tiberio Esparza—and of course, Jim Hyde—none of this would have happened. Triple thank yous, gentlemen!

And that leaves me wanting to thank every one of my new friends and colleagues. We are brothers forever . . . RawHyde! Lastly, we cannot end without thanking the author of this collection, Colin Evans, who rose to the occasion with wit, professionalism, and a busy pen. Thank you too, Colin!

—Alfonse Palaima